Beginners' Norwegian

Irene Burdese

Teach Yourself®

Beginners' Norwegian

Irene Burdese

First published in Great Britain in 2015 as *Get Started in Norwegian* by Hodder and Stoughton. An Hachette UK company.

This edition published by Teach Yourself in 2025
An imprint of John Murray Press

1

Editorial support from Haremi Ltd

A CIP catalogue record for this title is available from the British Library

Paperback ISBN 9781399821940
ebook ISBN 9781399821971

Typeset by Integra Software Services Pvt. Ltd., Pondicherry, India

Printed and bound in Great Britain by Clays Ltd, Elcograf S.p.A.

John Murray Press policy is to use papers that are natural, renewable and recyclable products and made from wood grown in sustainable forests. The logging and manufacturing processes are expected to conform to the environmental regulations of the country of origin.

John Murray Press
Carmelite House
50 Victoria Embankment
London EC4Y 0DZ

Teach Yourself
123 S. Broad St., Ste 2755
Philadelphia, PA, 19109

www.teachyourself.com

John Murray Press, part of Hodder & Stoughton Limited
An Hachette UK company

Contents

About the author

I was born in Italy, where I started studying English, French and German at a young age. I took both my Bachelor's and Master's degrees in Modern Foreign Languages and Literatures (English, German and Scandinavian languages) at the University of Turin, majoring in English. My Master's thesis is in English, Italian and Norwegian on comparative translations of Sigrid Undset's masterpiece *Kristin Lavransdatter*. I began studying Norwegian in Turin during my last year of high school, and I continued at university, where I also took some beginner Danish and Swedish language courses, as well as Scandinavian literature courses. Since my first year as a Bachelor's student, I have spent every summer in Norway, taking part in numerous summer courses held by several Norwegian universities, such as the International Summer School in Oslo, where I also took the **Test i norsk høyere nivå**, also known as **Bergenstest**. I spent my first year as a Master's student in Norway, participating in the Erasmus Programme, and taking courses both in Norwegian language and in English literary translation and English literature at the University of Oslo. During my second and last year as a Master's student, I was able to come back to the University of Oslo for three months to do research on Sigrid Undset for my thesis, under the supervision of academic and scholar Liv Bliksrud. The following year, I published an article based on my Master's thesis about the Italian translations of Sigrid Undset's *Kristin Lavransdatter* and its missing chapters. After the Master's, I took a one-year specialization course in literary translation and I started teaching English language and literature in high school in Italy. I also started teaching Norwegian to language students at the University of Turin, and I became a private tutor. With my colleague Cathrine Rysst, from UiO, I wrote the textbook *Lær deg norsk!*, an A1–B1 course, which is the first textbook especially designed for Italians learning Norwegian. It was published in Italy in January 2015. In 2017, I took the PPU (Praktisk Pedagogisk Utdanning) to become an authorized teacher in Norway, and I have been a teacher of English, Norwegian and Norwegian as a Second Language in high school in Norway since 2018.

Irene Burdese

How to use this book

This book consists of an introduction to the Norwegian language and a **Pronunciation guide** to familiarize you with the basic sounds of Norwegian. The core of the book are 10 units which will help you learn basic language function and introduce key topics for everyday communication.

A little goes a long way! Try to use the book little and often, rather than for long stretches at a time. This will help you to create a study habit, much in the same way you would a sport or music. Leave the book somewhere handy so that you can pick it up for just a few minutes.

Before you start, make a plan! Setting goals affects the programming of your brain, strengthening neural pathways and ultimately making it more likely that you will achieve those goals. Before you begin, think about how much time you want to devote to learning, which skills or areas you want to focus on, and identify specific ideas you want to be able to communicate or activities you want to engage in.

Track your progress! Start a notebook to use for study, where you can create vocabulary lists, a grammar summary, questions you'd like answered, etc. Keep track of your resources – films, podcasts, songs or blogs you like – and jot down a few words or expressions you may have recognized or learned. The more you can reflect on your learning process, the deeper your connection with the language will be. For guidance in this process, we recommend Teach Yourself's *Fluentish: Language Learning Planner & Journal*, published by Jo Franco.

Use the tools at the beginning of each unit to help you set goals, plan your time, and keep track of the work you do.

IN THIS UNIT, YOU WILL LEARN HOW TO

Each unit begins with an overview of the language you will be learning and skills you will be acquiring.

MY PROGRESS TRACKER

Use the progress tracker to plan your study time and to keep a record of what you've accomplished. The first column tracks time, and the remaining five columns represent the skills you'll be working on: listening, pronunciation, reading, writing, and spoken interaction.

Personalize the tracker: Instead of the date or day, you can enter an increment of time. Add columns for culture, vocabulary, grammar or any other area you wish to focus on. Give yourself a star when you feel you've done particularly well. Make it your own! Review your tracker regularly and see which areas could use more practice.

Use the **Self check** at the end of each unit to evaluate your progress.

Try to practice each skill every day.

The icons in the progress tracker are used throughout the book to help you easily identify and locate the skills you want to practice:

 Listening skills

 Speaking – pronunciation skills

 Reading skills

 Writing skills

 Speaking – conversation skills

Remember: there are many ways to build your skills in addition to those provided in this book: use a language-learning app, listen to music or podcasts, watch TV shows or movies, go to a restaurant, follow Norwegian social media accounts (there are wonderful teachers who post regularly), read blogs, newspapers or magazines, switch the language settings in your apps to Norwegian, or sign up for a language exchange or a tutor.

Units 1–10

The units open with a **cultural reading** in English and a **Vocabulary builder** page with thematic groupings of related words that can be studied together, as well as **new expressions** – specific words and expressions needed to understand the upcoming conversations or reading passages. You will often notice missing words in the Vocabulary builder. Look for patterns to help you complete the lists.

Dialogues are recorded conversations that you can listen to and practice, beginning with a narrative that helps you understand what you are going to hear, with a focusing question and follow-up activities. It is important to listen to or read this material at least twice; work out the meaning for yourself as far as you can, but use the lists of key words and phrases to help you. As in any conversation, listen for the meaning and don't worry about understanding each individual word. This will come with time. The **Norwegian–English Glossary** at the back of the book allows you to quickly access all the vocabulary that is presented in the course.

The **Language discovery** asks you to think about one or more aspects of the grammar seen in the Conversation. (See below for more information about the learning approach known as the Discovery method.) There are notes throughout to help guide you and draw your attention to interesting language or culture points.

The **Practice** sections give you the opportunity to try out the language that has been presented in the unit; each exercise focuses on listening, reading, writing and speaking. Finally, in every unit there is a short test – **Test yourself** – which enables you to check whether you can now do some of the language tasks covered by that unit. There are also three **Reviews**, after Units 3, 6 and 10, to help you consolidate what you've learned. You can check all your answers in the **Answer key** at the back of the book.

Revise each unit until you can do it without errors before you go on to the next unit. It is important to go back over material in areas where you are making errors, rather than carrying on regardless, which is bound to get you into trouble later.

How to be a successful language learner

The Discovery method

There are lots of philosophies and approaches to language learning, some practical, some quite unconventional, and far too many to list here. Perhaps you know of a few, or even have some techniques of your own. In this book we have incorporated the Discovery method of learning, a sort of DIY approach to language learning. What this means is that you will be encouraged throughout the course to engage your mind and figure out the language for yourself, through identifying patterns, understanding grammar concepts, noticing words that are similar to English, and more.

Simply put, if you figure something out for yourself, you're more likely to understand it. And when you use what you've learned, you're more likely to remember it. And because many of the essential but (let's admit it!) dull details, such as grammar rules, are introduced through the Discovery method, you'll have more fun while learning. Soon, the language will start to make sense and you'll be relying on your own intuition to construct original sentences independently, not just listening and repeating.

Everyone can succeed in learning a language – the key is to know how to learn it.

Learn to learn

There are many strategies that can help you become a successful language learner. Different people have different learning styles and some of these approaches will be more effective for you than others. Use this list as a point of inspiration when you want to find the most effective ways to advance your skills and begin your journey to fluency.

VOCABULARY

Words are the building blocks of language. The more you use the words you're introduced to, the more quickly they'll lodge into your memory. These study tips will help you remember better:

- Say the words out loud as you read them. Listen to the audio several times.
- Write the words over and over again. Create flash cards, drawings and mind maps.
- It helps to group new words in categories, like food or furniture, or according to the situations in which they occur, e.g. restaurant, hotel, sight-seeing, or their functions, e.g. greetings, parting, thanks, apologizing.
- Cover up the English side of the vocabulary list and see if you remember the meaning of the word. Then cover up the Norwegian side, and see if you can remember the word itself.
- Use mnemonic tricks for words with similar-sounding words in English.
- Post sticky notes for words for objects around your house.
- Pay attention to patterns in words, e.g. adding **-er** or **-ene** to the end of a noun indicates plurality.

GRAMMAR

Grammar gives your language structure. It allows you to experiment with the vocabulary you learn because you'll understand how they work together to create meaning. In other words, you'll begin to develop a feel for the language. Here are some tips to help you study more effectively:

- Write your own grammar glossary and add new information and examples as you go along.
- Experiment with grammar rules. Use old vocabulary to practice new grammar structures.
- Try to find examples of grammar in conversations or other articles.
- When you learn a new verb form, review other verbs you know that follow the same pattern.
- Compare Norwegian structures with your own language or other languages you may already speak. Try to find out some rules on your own and be ready to spot the exceptions.

PRONUNCIATION

The best way to improve your pronunciation is simply to practice as much as possible. Study individual sounds first, then full words and sentences. Don't forget, it's not just about pronouncing letters and words correctly, but using the right intonation. So, when practicing words and sentences, mimic the rising and falling intonation of Norwegian speakers.

- Repeat all of the conversations, line by line. Listen to yourself and try to mimic what you hear.
- Record yourself and compare yourself to the recordings.
- Make a list of words that give you trouble and practice them.

LISTENING AND READING

The conversations in this book include questions to help guide you in your understanding. But you can go further by following some of these tips.

- Imagine the situation. Try to imagine where the scene is taking place and who the main characters are. Let your experience of the world help you guess the meaning of the conversation, e.g. if a conversation takes place in a café, you can predict the kind of vocabulary that will be used.
- Concentrate on the main part. When watching a film in another language you usually get the meaning of the whole story from a few individual shots. Understanding a conversation or text in another language is similar. Concentrate on the main message and don't worry about individual words.
- Learn to cope with uncertainty – don't over-use your dictionary! You don't have to look up every word you don't know – try to deduce the meaning from the context. Concentrate on trying to get the gist of the passage and underline the words you don't understand. If after the third time there are still words which prevent you from getting the general meaning of the passage, look them up in the dictionary.

WRITING

You'll have plenty of writing practice using this book. Creating vocabulary lists, grammar summaries and taking good notes as you study is another great opportunity to practice writing.

If you're keeping your lists or notes on your smartphone, computer or tablet, remember to switch the keyboard language to be able to include all accents and special characters. Here are some other ways to practice writing:

- Write out the answers to all Practice and Test Yourself questions.
- Create your own vocabulary lists and a grammar summary.

- Look up writing prompts for language learning or try writing a daily gratitude journal in Norwegian.
- Write out your To Do and shopping lists in Norwegian.
- Join online forums and discussion groups about or in Norwegian.

SPEAKING

The greatest obstacle to speaking a new language is the fear of making a mistake. Keep in mind that you make mistakes in your own language – it's simply part of the human condition. Accept it. Most errors are not serious and they will not affect the meaning. So concentrate on getting your message across and use the mistakes as learning opportunities. Here are some useful tips to help you practice speaking Norwegian:

- Rehearse in Norwegian. Hold a conversation with yourself, using the conversations of the units as models and the structures you have learned previously.
- When you're going about your day, e.g. buying groceries, ordering food and drinks, do it in Norwegian in your mind! Look at objects around you and try to name them in Norwegian. Look at people around you and try to describe them in detail.
- Answer all of the questions in the book out loud. Say the dialogues out loud, then try to replace sentences with ones that are true for you. Try to role-play different situations in the book.
- Keep talking. The best way to improve your fluency in a language is to talk every time you have the opportunity to do so: keep the conversations flowing and don't worry about the mistakes. If you get stuck for a particular word, don't let the conversation stop; simplify what you want to say; paraphrase or replace the unknown word with one you do know.

Learning a language takes work. But the work can be a lot of fun! So, let's begin!

Kos deg med å lære norsk!

Enjoy learning Norwegian!

About the Norwegian language

Norwegian is a Scandinavian language, closely related to Danish and Swedish. Unlike those other Scandinavian countries, however, Norway does not have an official spoken standard, and Norwegians usually speak the dialect of their place of origin. There are two official written languages: **bokmål** and **nynorsk**.

Bokmål is closer to written Danish and is usually the written standard learners of Norwegian are taught. It must be stressed, however, that considerable variations are allowed within **bokmål** (and within **nynorsk**), depending largely on the user's choices between relatively more 'conservative' or 'liberal' spellings and grammar, or depending on the influence of an individual user's local dialect.

Many people use a more 'conservative' **bokmål**, choosing not to use the feminine gender of nouns but only the 'common gender', as in Danish. You will notice this in the book, by reading and listening to the dialogues. However, you will encounter many people who do use feminine nouns, and so they are present everywhere else in the book, since they are largely used when writing a more 'liberal' **bokmål**, also influenced by dialects. The vast majority of spoken dialects in Norway use all three genders (masculine, feminine and neuter), with the notable exception of Bergen, where the local dialect only uses the 'common gender' and the neuter gender.

Why learn Norwegian?

Learn Norwegian and you will be able to:

- communicate with around 5.5 million inhabitants of Norway;
- read Danish and make yourself understood by around 6 million inhabitants of Denmark;
- understand Swedish speakers and make yourself understood by around 10.5 million inhabitants of Sweden.

You should also be able to get by in Norwegian with the inhabitants of Iceland, meaning that they may understand you, while you might have some problems understanding them.

Even if there are fewer speakers of Norwegian than of other languages, learning a new language always gives an insight into the culture as well, bringing people together. Moreover, Norwegian is a musical language, so it is very beautiful.

Features of Norwegian

As mentioned above, Norwegian is a Scandinavian language. This means that after having learned Norwegian it is much easier to understand the other Scandinavian languages. Since it is also a Germanic language, like German and English, learning Norwegian may not be that difficult for English speakers.

For an English speaker it is often easy to guess the meaning of Norwegian words, but since there is no standard spoken Norwegian, sometimes it can be difficult to adjust at first. In terms of written Norwegian, for historical reasons there are two official languages: **bokmål** and **nynorsk**. Since Norway was in a union with Denmark until 1814, the upper class spoke Danish, while the people spoke dialect(s). After gaining independence from Denmark in 1814, Norwegians decided to abandon Danish as an official language and, by rendering it more Norwegian, they created **riksmål** first, and then **bokmål**. They also decided to create a new language, called **nynorsk** "new Norwegian", which is based on the similarities between the many dialects. Norwegians can learn both languages at school, but they get to decide which one will be their first choice. In some areas of Norway, especially on the west coast and in the north, it is more frequent to meet users of **nynorsk**. All official documents and laws in Norway are written both in **bokmål** and in **nynorsk**.

The variety of Norwegian that you will learn with this book is **bokmål**, and in terms of the spoken language, this course is based on the Oslo dialect, which is the closest to **bokmål**. This is the normal approach when learning Norwegian. As you progress and make contact with Norwegian speakers, you will notice that adjusting to the various dialects is not that difficult, especially because Norwegians are generally kind enough to normalize their speech and explain the most difficult terms when they find out that you are learning the language.

Norwegian grammar

Norwegian grammar differs from English grammar in some notable ways:

- verbs have the same form for every person (there is no *-s* in the third person);
- there are three genders, masculine, feminine and neuter, and adjectives are declined following the gender of the noun, if it is singular, or take a special ending if the noun is plural;
- some people still do not use any feminine words (because Danish does not have the feminine), so all feminine words can also be masculine.

This may sound confusing and difficult at first, but really it is not. And once you learn the rules, you will see that speaking correct Norwegian is not difficult at all.

Stress and accent

Norwegian, like Swedish, is a tone language, which means that more than one tone may be used in words that contain more than one syllable. That is why Norwegian is such a musical language. In Norwegian there are two such word pitch accents: 'single tone' (also called *toneme 1* or *one-syllable pitch accent*) and 'double tone' (also called *toneme 2* or *two-syllable pitch accent*). Some Norwegian words are written the same, or differ from one another only by one letter, but their meaning changes according to the pitch accent: **bønder** (*farmers*) – **bønner** (*prayers*); **endene** (*ducks*) – **endene** (*ends*). Moreover, Norwegian has *word stress* (different syllables in words are stressed) and *sentence stress* (the words that are most significant for the meaning are stressed). Tone languages are not very common among Indo-European languages, so this may be a bit difficult, but the trick is to always listen carefully and imitate the pronunciation.

Vocabulary building

Since Norwegian and English are both Germanic languages, they share many similar words and so guessing their meaning can be fun and useful.

For instance, the word **mann** means *man*, the verb **gå** means *to go*, **komme** means *to come*, and so on.

There are also many false friends, though; for example: **spill** is the imperative of *play*, **smell** means *crash*, **her** means *here*, **fart** means *speed* and **men** means *but*.

Finnmark
Troms
Nordland
Trøndelag
Møre og Romsdal
Innlandet
Vestland
Buskerud
Akershus
Oslo
Telemark
Østfold
Rogaland
Agder
Vestfold

Pronunciation guide

As mentioned earlier, Norwegian is a Scandinavian language, closely related to Danish and Swedish. As with the latter, Norwegian is also a tone language, so it sounds like a melody. Although Norwegian and Danish are closely related, it is far easier to speak Norwegian and understand Norwegians, even if they are speaking a dialect. In order to become used to the different dialects, you can listen to the radio (NRK has a free app, which allows you to listen to several radio channels for free), watch Norwegian movies and TV programs, and listen to Norwegian music. When you are in Norway you should try and practice as much as you can, although Norwegians are quite fluent in English, and you will have to ask them to speak Norwegian instead of English to help you practice.

Alphabet

00.01 The Norwegian alphabet has 29 letters. Their names (in brackets) are used when spelling words out loud.

A, a	(a)	**P, p**	(pe)
B, b	(be)	**Q, q**	(ku)
C, c	(se)	**R, r**	(ærr)
D, d	(de)	**S, s**	(ess)
E, e	(e)	**T, t**	(te)
F, f	(eff)	**U, u**	(u)
G, g	(ge)	**V, v**	(ve)
H, h	(hå)	**W, w**	(dobbelt ve)
I, i	(i)	**X, x**	(eks)
J, j	(je) or (jodd)	**Y, y**	(y)
K, k	(kå)	**Z, z**	(sett)
L, l	(ell)	**Æ, æ**	(æ)
M, m	(emm)	**Ø, ø**	(ø)
N, n	(enn)	**Å, å**	(å)
O, o	(u)		

VOWELS

00.02 The last three letters in the alphabet are vowels, as is the letter **y**, so this means that Norwegian has nine vowels altogether: **a**, **e**, **i**, **o**, **u**, **y**, **æ**, **ø**, **å**; but all vowels can be both short and long, so this means that there are 18 actual sounds.

Usually a vowel is short when it comes before two consonants, and it is long when it comes before one consonant, or none.

Letter	Pronunciation variety	Examples
a	Short, same sound as the English 'a' in *cat*. Long, same sound as the English 'a' in *father*.	**takk** (*thanks*), **katt** (*cat*), **matte** (*rug*) **tak** (*roof*), **far** (*father*), **fat** (*bowl*)
e	Short, same as the English 'e' in *pen* and *men*. Long, same sound as in the short, but stretched out, a little like 'e' in *ear*.	**renn** (*race*), **penn** (*pen*), **sent** (*late*), **menn** (*men*), **legge** (*to set*) **ren** (*clean*), **pen** (*beautiful*), **sen** (*late*), **men** (*but*), **lege** (*doctor*)
i	Short, like the 'i' in the English *bin* and *kiss*. Long, similar to the English 'ee' in *see* or 'ea' in *sea* and *heat*.	**tillatelse** (*permit*), **minne** (*to remind*), **fint** (*well / nice*) **til** (*to*), **mine** (*my*), **fine** (*nice*)
o	Short, like the English 'oo' in *book*, but a shorter sound. Sometimes pronounced as the English 'o' in *gone*, especially when the vowel is followed by two (identical) consonants. Long, like the English 'oo' in *moon*.	**ost** (*cheese*), **Oslo**, **bodde** (*lived*), **hvor** (*where*) **komme** (*to come*), **dronning** (*queen*), **konge** (*king*) **bok** (*book*), **bor** (*live, lives*), **bo** (*to live*), **pose** (*plastic bag*)
u	No English equivalent. Short, start with the 'u' sound in *true*, but round the lips very tightly. Also similar to the final vowel in *new*, but shorter. Long, start with the 'u' sound in *true*, but round the lips very tightly. Also similar to the final vowel in *new*.	**huske** (*remember*), **buss** (*bus*), **busk** (*bush*), **hund** (*dog*), **du** (*you*) **hus** (*house*), **frue** (*madam*), **bue** (*bow*)
y	No English equivalent. The sound is between a Norwegian 'i' and a Norwegian 'u'. Short, pronounced with rounded lips. Long, pronounced with tightly rounded lips.	**bytte** (*exchange*), **hylle** (*shelf*), **sykle** (*to cycle*) **ny** (*new*), **by** (*city*), **hyle** (*scream*), **sy** (*sew*)
æ	Short, similar to the English 'a' in *bad*. Long, similar to the English 'a' in *bad*, but stretched.	**færre** (*fewer*) **være** (*to be*), **været** (*weather*)

ø	No English equivalent. Similar to the German 'ö' or the French 'eu'.	Short **ørret** (*trout*), **bøtte** (*bucket*), **rømme** (*sour cream*) Long **øret** (*the ear*), **løpe** (*to run*), **fløte** (*cream*), **kjøpe** (*to buy*)
å	Short, like the 'o' in *Scot*. Long, similar to the English sound 'aw' in *saw*.	**flått** (*tick*), **gått** (*gone*), **blått** (*blue* – neuter) **håpe** (*to hope*), **gå** (*to go*), **blå** (*blue*)

DIPHTHONGS

00.03 Some combinations of vowels form a diphthong, which is two vowels pronounced together. Norwegian diphthongs have no English equivalent.

Diphthong	Pronunciation variety	Examples
ei	Similar to the 'a' in *babe*, or the sound of the word *eye*.	**lei** (*sad / sorry*), **sei** (*coley*), **vei** (*street*), **leilighet** (*apartment*), **hei** (*hi*)
ai	Like the 'i' in *vine*.	**hai** (*shark*), **mai** (*May*), **kai** (*quay*)
øy	The first sound is similar to the German 'ö' or the French 'eu', while the 'y' is similar to the English *kiss* or *bin*.	**bøye** (*bend*), **gøy** (*funny*), **fornøyelse** (*amusement*), **øye** (*eye*), **øy** (*isle*), **høy** (*high*)
au, eu	Similar to 'ou' in *mouse*, but the 'u' is similar to the final vowel sound in *new*.	**august** (*August*), **Europa** (*Europe*), **auksjon** (*auction*), **maur** (*ant*), **Australia** (*Australia*), **pause** (*break*), **euro** (*Euro*), **sau** (*sheep*)

CONSONANTS

00.04 The letters **c**, **q**, **w**, **x**, **z** are only used in words (e.g. **quiz**, **xylofon**, etc.) and names (e.g. **Christian**, **William**, etc.) imported from other languages and are not common.

Letter	Pronunciation variety	Examples
b	As the English 'b' in *bed*.	**banan** (*banana*), **bare** (*just*), **bra** (*good, well*), **bedre** (*better*), **blomster** (*flower*)
c	As the English 'c' in *car*, used only in loans from other languages and in first names.	**camembert** (*Camembert*)

d	Hard 'd' as in the English *dad*. 'd' is silent in the combinations **-ld**, **-nd**, **-rd** and at the end of a word, when it is preceded by a vowel.	**Danmark**, **danne** (*create*), **dame** (*woman*), **dele** (*share*) **Trondheim**, **bord** (*table*), **med** (*with*), **kald** (*cold*)
f	As the English 'f' in *fire*.	**fire** (*four*), **fem** (*five*)
g	Hard 'g' as in the English *girl*. In some combinations, such as **-gi**, **-gei**, **-gy**, 'g' can also be pronounced as the 'y' in *you*. 'g' is silent when a word ends in the combination **-ig** and begins with the combination **gj-**. In some loan words the 'g' becomes similar to the sound 'sh' in *shoe*.	**galskap** (*madness*), **gå** (*to go*), **gidde** (*have the strength to do something*) **gi** (*to give*), **gikk** (*went*), **gifte** (*to marry*), **geit** (*goat*), **gyldig** (*valid*) **hyggelig** (*pleasant*), **billig** (*cheap*), **vanskelig** (*difficult*), **gjerne** (*gladly*), **gjennom** (*through*), **gjøre** (*to do*) **giro** (*money transfer*), **generelt** (*generally*), **regi** (*direction*)
h	Always pronounced before a vowel. Never pronounced before **-v-** and **-j-**.	**hals** (*neck*), **hund** (*dog*), **hatt** (*hat*) **hvem** (*who*), **hvor** (*where*), **hva** (*what*), **hvordan** (*how*), **hjelpe** (*help*), **hjerne** (*brain*)
j	Close to the sound of the English 'y'.	**ja** (*yes*), **jeg** (*I*), **jakke** (*jacket*), **jeger** (*hunter*)
k	Like 'k' in the English *keep* before most of the vowels and consonants. The combinations **kj-**, **ki-**, and **ky-** are pronounced like 'ch' in *Charles* with a mild initial 't' sound.	**kniv** (*knife*), **kar** (*guy*), **komme** (*come*), **kan** (*can*), **kunde** (*client*), **kvinne** (*woman*) **kino** (*cinema*), **kirke** (*church*), **kjenne** (*to know*), **kjøpe** (*to buy*), **kjøre** (*to drive*), **kylling** (*chicken*), **kysse** (*to kiss*)
l	As the English 'l' in *leave*.	**lure** (*to wonder*), **leve** (*to live*), **laks** (*salmon*), **lede** (*to lead*)
m	As the English 'm' in *mother*.	**måned** (*month*), **mor** (*mother*), **male** (*to paint*), **måle** (*to measure*)
n	As the English 'n' in *no*. The combination **-ng** and sometimes **-nk** is pronounced as the English 'ng' in *thing*.	**nabo** (*neighbor*), **nonne** (*nun*), **Norge** (*Norway*), **nei** (no) **ting** (*thing*), **sang** (*song*), **lang** (*long*), **bank**, **mange** (*many*)
p	As the English 'p' in *pen*.	**prest** (*priest*), **presis** (*timely*), **panne** (*pan*), **poeng** (*point*), **penn** (*pen*)
q	As the English 'k'.	**quiz** (*quiz*)

r	A rolled 'r' made with the tip of the tongue. (In the south of Norway, especially the Kristiansand area, and in the Bergen area, it is not rolled but made with the root of the tongue at the back of the mouth.) The combination **-rs-** is pronounced like 'sh' in *mash*. The combinations **-rt**, **-rd**, **-rl** and **-rn** create a particular sound, made by bending the tip of the tongue backwards and making it slightly touch the palate at the back of the front teeth.	**rastløs** (*restless*), **rolig** (*calm*), **reagere** (*to react*), **rote** (*to disarray*) **kurs** (*course*), **Lars**, **norsk** (*Norwegian*) **barn** (*child*), **bort** (*away*), **fjern** (*far*), **forteller** (*tell*), **gjerne** (*gladly*), **gjort** (*done*), **hvordan** (*how*), **port** (*gate*), **ærlig** (*sincere*)
s	Never voiced, so like the 's' sound in *sun*. An 's' on its own cannot give a 'sh' sound, but it does give the sound 'sh' in the combinations **-sl**, **skj-**, **sj-** and **sk** + **y**, **i**, **ei**, **øy**.	**stol** (*chair*), **sur** (*sour / angry*), **sild** (*herring*), **søndag** (*Sunday*), **seks** (*six*) **sjal** (*shawl*), **sjel** (*soul*), **sjelden** (*seldom*), **ski** (*ski*), **skinke** (*ham*), **skjema** (*scheme*), **skjære** (*to slice*), **sky** (*cloud*), **skøyter** (*skater*), **sliten** (*tired*), **stasjon** (*station*)
t	Pronounced like the English 't' in *tooth*. 't' at the end of a singular neuter noun is never pronounced, as well as at the end of the neuter pronoun **det**. The final 't' is always pronounced at the end of verbs in the past tense, neuter adjectives, non-neuter nouns and adverbs. In some cases, the combination **tj-** can be pronounced like 'ch' in *Charles* with a mild initial 't' sound right before the 'y' sound. In other cases, the combination **tj-** is pronounced as it is written, so with a hard 't' sound right before the 'y' sound.	**tann** (*tooth*), **tre** (*three*), **trær** (*trees*), **tante** (*aunt*), **ting** (*thing*) **barnet** (*the child*), **brødet** (*the bread*), **det** (*it*), **flyet** (*the plane*), **hjemmet** (*the home*), **huset** (*the house*), **skapet** (*the closet*), **været** (*the weather*) **snakket** (*talked*), **godt** (*well*), **nytt** (*new* – neuter), **svart** (*black*), **leilighet** (*apartment*) **tjue** (*twenty*), **tjukk** (*thick*) **tjene** (*earn*), **tjeneste** (*service / favor*)
v	Like the English 'v' in *very*.	**været** (*the weather*), **vann** (*water*), **venn** (*friend*), **venninne** (*female friend*), **visdom** (*wisdom*), **visum** (*passport*), **veldig** (*very*)

w	Like 'v' in *very*. It only occurs in names and words of non-Norwegian origin.	**waliser** (*Welsh*)
x	Like 'ks', never like 'gz' as in *example*. It only occurs in names and words of non-Norwegian origin.	**xylofon** (*xylophone*), **sex** (*sex*)
z	Like voiceless 's' in *see*. It only occurs in names and words of non-Norwegian origin.	**zirkon** (*zircon*), **zoolog** (*zoologist*)

1

In this unit, you will learn how to:

» say *hello* and *goodbye*.
» introduce yourself and others.
» say where you come from and where you live.
» use personal pronouns and verbs in the present tense.

Hei! Hyggelig å treffe deg!

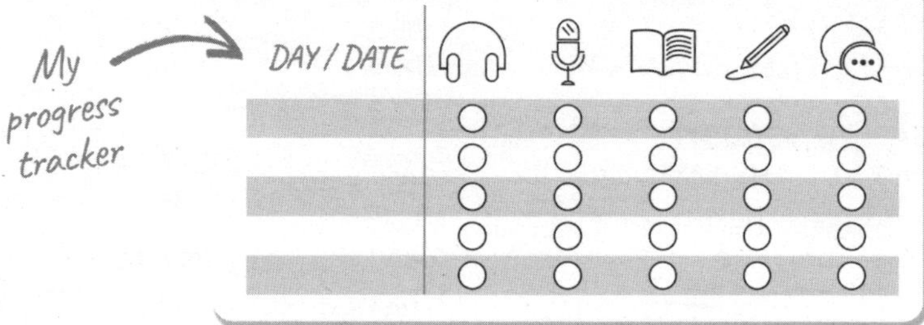

Greetings

Hei, **heisann** and **hallo** are the expressions that are most frequently used when meeting someone. The expression **ha det bra**, or simply **ha det**, is used when saying goodbye. None of these expressions or phrases are particularly formal, but can be used with people we do not know very well. **God morgen** is slightly more formal, and can only be used in the morning, while **god dag** can be used all day. It is also possible to use this expression when leaving, simply by adding **å ha** (*to have*): **ha en god dag**. If it is evening, one says **god kveld**, while **god natt** is only used when wishing someone good night.

Norwegians have a particular way of greeting each other when they meet again: depending on how long it has been since they last met, they can say **takk for sist** or **takk for i går**. They also use these kinds of expressions when saying *goodbye*. Again, depending on the time of the day, they can choose from **takk for i dag / i kveld / i natt**; and they can use **takk for meg** or **takk for nå** at the end of a lecture or a speech.

Norwegian people say takk for maten after they finish a meal that someone else has cooked. What do you think this means?

Vocabulary builder

01.01 Listen to the following phrases and expressions, and then try to imitate the Norwegian pronunciation. Complete the missing English translations.

GREETINGS

Hei! / Heisann! / Hallo!	*Hi! / Hello! (less formal)*
God dag!	______
God morgen!	______
God kveld! / God aften!	______
Takk for sist!	*Thank you for last time.*
Takk for i går!	*Thank you for yesterday.*

SAYING GOODBYE

Ha det bra! / Ha det fint! / Ha det godt! / Ha det!	*Goodbye!*
På gjensyn!	*Goodbye! (more formal; lit. See you again)*
Vi ses! / Vi sees!	______
God natt!	______
Takk for i dag!	*Thank you for today.*
Takk for maten!	______

LANGUAGE TIP

Takk for alt is a false friend. It literally means *thanks for everything* but is really only used to say *rest in peace*. Norwegians who do not know you are a learner might be upset if you use it.

NEW EXPRESSIONS

Some of these new expressions are used in the following dialogues. Note their meanings and the differences between the various alternatives.

Hva heter du?	*What's your name?*
Jeg heter ...	*My name is ...*
Hvor kommer du fra?	*Where are you from?*
Jeg kommer fra ...	*I'm from ...*
Hvordan går det?	*How is it going?*
Det går bra / fint / ikke så bra / dårlig, takk.	*It's going well / fine / not so fine / badly, thanks.*
Hvordan har du det?	*How are you?*

Jeg har det bra / fint / ikke så bra / dårlig, takk.	*I'm well / fine / not so fine / bad, thanks.*
Hyggelig å hilse på deg!	*Nice to meet you!*
Hyggelig å treffe deg igjen!	*Nice to see you again!*
I like måte.	*Likewise. (lit. For me as well.)*
Tusen takk!	*Thank you very much. (lit. a thousand thanks)*

Dialogue 1

01.02 Listen carefully to the conversation before answering the questions.

1 Where is the conversation taking place?

2 Have the speakers met before?

Sven	Hei, jeg heter Sven. Hva heter du?
Marit	Hyggelig å hilse på deg Sven, jeg heter Marit. Hvor kommer du fra?
Sven	Jeg kommer fra Tromsø. Hvor kommer du fra?
Marit	Jeg kommer fra Lillehammer. Hvor bor du?
Sven	Jeg bor i Oslo på Grønland, hvor bor du?
Marit	Jeg bor også i Oslo, men på Vinderen.
Sven	Hva studerer du?
Marit	Jeg studerer nordisk språk og litteratur, og du?
Sven	Jeg studerer lingvistikk.

3 What phrases do the speakers use to introduce themselves? Match the Norwegian with the English translation.

a Hyggelig å møte deg. **1** Nice to see you.
b Hyggelig å hilse på deg. **2** Nice meeting you.
c Hyggelig å treffe deg. **3** Nice making your acquaintance.
d Hyggelig å se deg. **4** Nice meeting you.

4 Where does Sven come from?

5 Where does Marit come from?

6 Re-read the dialogue and answer the following questions.

a Where does Sven live?

1 Tromsø **2** Oslo

b Where does Marit live?
   1 Oslo
   2 Lillehammer
c What does Marit study?
   1 nordisk språk og litteratur
   2 lingvistikk
d What does Sven study?
   1 nordisk språk og litteratur
   2 lingvistikk

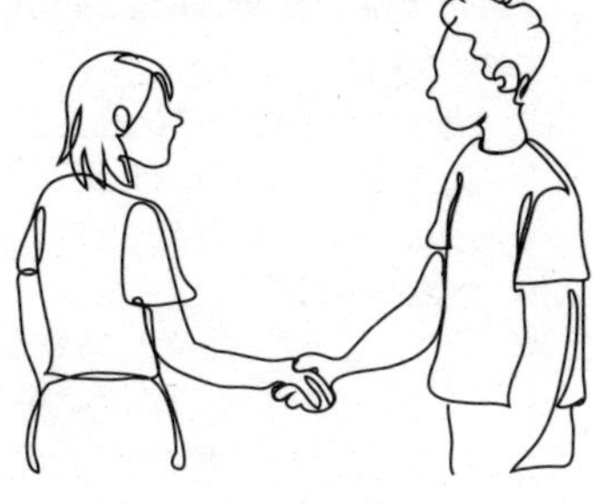

7 Fill in the blanks with the missing verbs.

a Jeg _______ Sven.

b Han _______ fra Tromsø.

8 Fill in the blanks with the missing pronouns.

a Hvor kommer _______ fra? (*you*, singular)

b _______ heter Marit. (*she*)

Language discovery 1

1 PERSONAL PRONOUNS

Personal pronouns are used to replace a noun or a name. Personal pronouns in Norwegian do not need the capital letter unless they are at the beginning of a sentence.

Subject		Object	
jeg	*I*	**meg**	*me*
du	*you*	**deg**	*you*
han	*he*	**ham/han**	*him*
hun	*she*	**henne**	*her*
den (non-neuter) **det** (neuter)	*it*	**den** **det**	*it*
vi	*we*	**oss**	*us*
dere	*you*	**dere**	*you*
de	*they*	**dem**	*them*

LANGUAGE TIP

Hen comes from the Swedish **hen**, which comes from the Finnish **hän**. It is used to talk about a person whose gender is unknown, or for non-binary people.

Examples:

Hen er ikke-binær. (*They are non-binary.*)

Eleven sier hen er syk i dag. (*The pupil/student say they are ill today.*)

1 Fill in the blanks with the missing pronouns from the right-hand column.

a	Hyggelig å hilse på _______. (*you*, plural)	**1**	jeg
b	_______ heter Sven. (*I*)	**2**	du
c	_______ heter Sven og Marit. (*we*)	**3**	han
d	Hva heter _______? (*you*, singular)	**4**	hun
e	_______ heter Sven. (*he*)	**5**	vi
f	_______ bor i Oslo. (*they*)	**6**	dere
g	_______ heter Marit. (*she*)	**7**	de

2 Read the following examples of personal pronouns used with å hete, å være, å treffe, å møte, å snakke, then answer the following questions.

Jeg heter Sven.	*My name is Sven. (lit. I am called Sven.)*
Hun heter Marit.	*Her name is Marit.*
Han er lærer.	*He is a teacher.*
Hun er ingeniør.	*She is an engineer.*
Jeg treffer deg i ettermiddag.	*I'll meet you this afternoon.*
Jeg møter henne i ettermiddag.	*I'll meet her this afternoon.*
Du snakker med meg.	*You speak with me. / You talk to me.*

a Would you use **jeg** or **meg** when translating the sentence *She is with me*?

b Would you use **hun** or **henne** when translating the sentence *I met her last night*?

2 VERBS IN THE PRESENT TENSE

Norwegian verbs in the present tense end in **-r**. Some simply take the **-r** at the end, while others lose an **-e** as well as the **å**: the *to* of the infinitive form.

(å bo)	**Jeg bor i Oslo.**	*I live in Oslo.*
(å komme)	**Du kommer fra London.**	*You come from London.*
(å bo)	**Vi bor i Norge.**	*We live in Norway.*
(å vente)	**Jeg venter på trikken.**	*I am waiting for the tram.*
(å jobbe)	**Vi jobber sammen.**	*We work together.*
(å hete)	**Hun heter Maja.**	*Her name is Maja.*
(å gjøre)	**Jeg gjør det.**	*I do / am doing it.*

Some verbs are irregular, since the *to* form is different from the present tense, such as **å være** (*to be*):

Abby er min venninne.	*Abby* ***is*** *my (female) friend.*
Erlend er min kollega.	*Erlend* ***is*** *my colleague.*
Abby er lærer.	*Abby* ***is*** *a teacher.*

3 Read the following description, paying attention to the words below it. Verbs are the same for all people. Then try to rewrite it in the third person.

> **Jeg heter Maja, jeg er norsk, jeg bor i Norge og jeg jobber i Oslo. Jeg har en hund og en katt. Jeg går ut, treffer venner og snakker med dem. Jeg liker Norge.**
> *My name is Maja, I am Norwegian, I live in Norway and I work in Oslo. I have a dog and a cat. I go out, meet some friends and chat with them. I like Norway.*

Heter (*have a name*), **er** (*am, is, are*), **bor** (*live, lives*), **jobber** (*work, works*), **har** (*have, has*), **går** (*go, goes*), **snakker** (*talk, talks / speak, speaks*), **liker** (*like, likes*).

Dialogue 2

01.03 *Maja Andresen and her colleague Erlend Våge are walking in the city center where they meet Abby Becker, a friend of Maja, at the tram station. Listen carefully to the dialogue before answering the questions.*

1 **Do Abby and Erlend know each other?**

2 **Where does Abby come from?**

Maja	Abby? Så hyggelig å se deg igjen! Hva gjør du her?
Abby	Hei! Lenge siden sist! Jeg er ferdig på jobb og venter på trikken.
Maja	Erlend, dette er min venninne Abby Becker, hun er lærer.
Erlend	Hyggelig å hilse på deg Abby.
Abby	I like måte.
Erlend	Hvor kommer du fra?
Abby	Jeg kommer fra London, men jeg bor i Oslo.
Erlend	Du er veldig flink i norsk!
Abby	Takk! Trikken kommer, vi sees snart. Ha det bra!

3 Read the conversation again and answer the questions.

a What is Abby doing there?
b What does Abby do for a living?
c Where does Abby live?
d What does Erlend tell Abby at the end?

4 **Look at the conversation again, then match the Norwegian with the English translation.**

a Så hyggelig å se deg igjen!
b Hva gjør du her?
c Dette er min venninne Abby Becker.
d Du er veldig flink i norsk!
  1 What are you doing here?
  2 Nice seeing you again!
  3 You are very good at speaking Norwegian!
  4 This is my friend Abby Becker.

5 **Find how Abby says the following in the conversation.**

a I have finished working and I am waiting for the tram.
b I come from London, but I live in Oslo.
c The tram is coming!

6 **Maja, Erlend and Abby ask each other questions. What words do they use for the following?**

a What
  1 hva **2** hvor **3** hvordan
b Where
  1 hva **2** hvor **3** hvordan

7 **What do you think veldig means?**

8 **What do you think flink means?**

Language discovery 2

ASKING AND ANSWERING QUESTIONS

In the following table, you can find Norwegian words used in questions and answers:

Spørreord	Question word
hva	*what*
hvem	*who*
hvor	*where*
hvordan	*how*
Hvorfor?...fordi	*why?...because*

når	*when*
hvilken	*which (m / f)*
hvilket	*which (n)*
hvilke	*which (plural)*
hvor mye	*how much*
hvor mange	*how many*

1 Now read those words being used in questions.

Hva heter du?	*What is your name?*
Hvor bor du?	*Where do you live?*
Hvordan har du det?	*How are you?*
Hvor kommer du fra?	*Where are you from?*
Hva gjør du her?	*What are you doing here?*
Er du norsk?	*Are you Norwegian?*
Har han en hund?	*Does he have a dog?*

2 Look at the two examples of questions with and without question words then choose the correct translations for the following questions.

***Hvor* kommer du fra?**	*Where are you from?*
Kommer du fra Oslo?	*Do you come from Oslo?*

a Bor du i Oslo?	**1** Are you from Cardiff?
b Hvor bor du?	**2** Where do you live?
c Heter du Marit?	**3** What are you doing?
d Hvordan har du det?	**4** Is your name Marit?
e Kommer du fra Cardiff?	**5** How are you?
f Hva gjør du?	**6** What is your name?
g Hva heter du?	**7** Do you live in Oslo?

Practice

1 Read Dialogue 2 again, then rearrange the following translations of Abby, Maja and Erlend's parts so that they are in the correct order.

Abby	Hi! Long time no see! I have finished working and I'm waiting for the tram.
Abby	I'm from London, but I live in Oslo.
Abby	Likewise.
Abby	Thanks! The tram is coming, see you soon. Bye!
Erlend	Nice meeting you, Abby.
Erlend	Where are you from?
Erlend	Your Norwegian is very good!
Maja	Abby? So nice to see you again! What are you doing here?
Maja	Erlend, this is my friend Abby Becker, she's a teacher.

2 Read the following summary and answer the questions.

Kjersti og Ella er venninner, de sitter på kafé og snakker sammen. Lars, en gammel venn av Kjersti, kommer og hilser på Ella. Lars er biolog og jobber ved Universitetet i Oslo. Ella er skuespiller og kommer fra Trondheim. Kjersti jobber også ved Universitetet i Oslo, hun er kjemiker og hun driver med forskning der.

- **a** Who are Kjersti and Ella?
- **b** Who is Lars?
- **c** Where does Lars work and what does he do there?
- **d** Where does Ella come from?
- **e** What does Ella do for a living?
- **f** Where does Kjersti work and what does she do there?

3 Look at the last sentence in the above text; how do you say *also / as well* in Norwegian?

Test yourself

1 Rearrange the words into sentences; don't forget to place the capital letter on the first word.

a	ham	snakker	med	hun	.
b	du	det	hvordan	har	?
c	Frankrike	fra	du	kommer	?
d	Norge	og	biolog	bor	jeg
	i	er	.		
e	heter	hva	dere	?	

2 What would you say in the following situations?

a when you meet a new acquaintance
b when you meet a friend you have not seen in a while
c to your friend, when you go away
d in the morning, when you arrive at the office

3 How do you ask the following questions?

a How are you?
b What is your name?
c Where are you from?
d How is it going?

4 Insert the correct verb from the right-hand column.

a	Jeg _______ Hanne.	**1**	bor
b	Han _______ fra USA.	**2**	er
c	Vi _______ ham.	**3**	heter
d	Hun _______ flink i norsk.	**4**	kommer
e	Jeg _______ på trikken.	**5**	treffer
f	Han _______ i Oslo.	**6**	venter

SELF CHECK

	I CAN ...
○	... say *hello* and *goodbye*.
○	... introduce myself and others.
○	... say where I come from and where I live.
○	... use personal pronouns and verbs in the present tense.

2

In this unit, you will learn how to:

» ask and answer (negative) questions.
» answer yes / no questions.
» talk about what you are doing now.
» talk about what language(s) you speak.
» say you (do not) want (to do) something.

Hvilket språk snakker du nå?

My progress tracker

DAY / DATE	Listening	Speaking	Reading	Writing	Conversation
	○	○	○	○	○
	○	○	○	○	○
	○	○	○	○	○
	○	○	○	○	○
	○	○	○	○	○

Official languages in Norway

While there is no standard spoken Norwegian, the two varieties of written Norwegian, **bokmål** and **nynorsk**, are both official languages and are used in official documents and laws. Norwegians can learn both languages at school, being able to choose freely which one they will use. Only 10–15 per cent of the population choose **nynorsk**, but there are some **kommuner** (*city councils*) where it is the first language. Since there is no standard official spoken Norwegian, everyone can speak their own dialect. Norwegians from different areas do not usually have big problems understanding each other, but it can be a challenge for non-Norwegian speakers. In those cases, students are usually taught the Oslo dialect, or a variety of Norwegian spoken in the surrounding area, which is more similar to written **bokmål**.

In Norway, people speak **norsk** (*Norwegian*), and **samisk** (*Sami*) in some northern regions, and it is not unusual for Norwegians to understand both **dansk** (*Danish*) and **svensk** (*Swedish*), and sometimes **islandsk** (*Icelandic*) and **færøysk** (*Faroese*). The majority of Norwegians speak very good **engelsk** (*English*). Nowadays many people in Norway also speak **polsk** (*Polish*) and **arabisk** (*Arabic*).

There are two possible endings for the names of languages. Can you tell what they are?

Vocabulary builder

02.01 **Listen to the following words, trying to imitate the Norwegian pronunciation. Then complete with the missing translations in English.**

LANGUAGES

walisisk	*Welsh*
tysk	*German*
svensk	_______
spansk	_______
skotsk	_______
samisk	_______
russisk	_______
portugisisk	_______
polsk	_______
norsk	_______
nederlandsk	_______
kinesisk	*Chinese*
italiensk	_______
islandsk	_______
irsk	_______
hindi	_______
fransk	_______
finsk	_______
færøysk	_______
engelsk	_______
dansk	_______
arabisk	_______

NATIONALITIES

amerikaner	________
danske	________
engelskmann	________
finne	________
franskmann	________
inder	________
ire	________
islending	________
italiener	________
kineser	*Chinese*
nederlender	________
nordmann	________
polakk	________
portugiser	________
russer	________
skotte	________
spanjol	________
sveitser	________
svenske	________
tysker	*German*
waliser	*Welshman / Welshwoman*
østerriker	________

NEW EXPRESSIONS

Some of these expressions are used in the following dialogues. Note their meaning and the differences between the various alternatives.

Hvilke språk snakker du?	*What languages do you speak?*
Jeg snakker norsk, italiensk og engelsk.	*I speak Norwegian, Italian and English.*
Hvilket språk snakker du?	*What language are you speaking?*
Jeg snakker norsk nå.	*I am speaking Norwegian now.*
Hvilken type hund er det?	*What kind of dog is that?*
Hvilken lampe liker du?	*What lamp do you like?*

1 How do we say *what / which* **in Norwegian?**

2 **Look at the following examples, and choose whether** *what / which* **is feminine / masculine, neuter or plural.**

a Hvilken lampe liker du?

b Hvilket språk snakker du?

c Hvilken hund har du?

d Hvilke språk snakker du?

Dialogue 1

02.02 **Listen carefully to Haakon and Stine talking about what languages they and their friends can speak.**

1 **Which languages do Haakon and Stine both speak?**

2 **Which language does Stine not speak?**

Stine	Hvilke språk snakker du?
Haakon	Jeg snakker norsk, fransk, tysk, engelsk og italiensk. Hva med deg?
Stine	Jeg snakker også norsk, fransk og engelsk, og jeg forstår litt tysk, men jeg snakker ikke italiensk.
Haakon	Det er mange språk, du er flink! Jeg har en venninne som snakker japansk og kinesisk, hun er veldig flink.
Stine	Å, så bra, de er vanskelige! Hvor bor hun?
Haakon	Hun kommer fra Norge, men hun bor i Tokyo nå.
Stine	Så flott! Kjenner du noen som snakker hindi?
Haakon	Nei, det gjør jeg ikke, hvorfor spør du?
Stine	Fordi jeg har lyst til å lære meg det, men jeg vet ikke om det er vanskelig.
Haakon	Jeg tror det er vanskelig, men du kan godt prøve. Du er flink i språk og du lærer sikkert fort.
Stine	Takk, du er snill!
Haakon	Nå må jeg gå, jeg har en avtale med en venn, jeg lærer ham norsk og han lærer meg portugisisk.
Stine	Å så smart! Vi sees, ha det.
Haakon	Ha det!

3 Re-read the dialogue and answer the following questions.

a What language does Stine want to learn?

b Why does she want to meet someone who speaks that language?

c What language is Haakon learning in exchange for teaching Norwegian?

4 Look at the conversation again, then match the Norwegian with the English translation.

a Jeg snakker også norsk, fransk og engelsk, og jeg forstår litt tysk, men jeg snakker ikke italiensk.

b Kjenner du noen som snakker hindi?

c Takk, du er snill!

d Fordi jeg har lyst til å lære meg det, men jeg vet ikke om det er vanskelig.

1 Thanks, you're kind.

2 I too speak Norwegian, French and English, and I understand a little German, but I don't speak Italian.

3 Because I want to learn it, but I don't know whether it's difficult.

4 Do you know anyone who speaks Hindi?

5 How do Haakon and Stine say the following?

a fantastic

1 smart 2 flott 3 fort

b quickly

1 flott 2 smart 3 fort

c intelligent, clever

1 flott 2 smart 3 fort

6 Choose the correct translation for the following expressions with *to teach* and *to learn*.

a I teach him Norwegian.

1 Jeg har lyst til å lære norsk.

2 Jeg lærer meg norsk.

3 Jeg lærer ham norsk.

b I am learning Norwegian.

1 Jeg har lyst til å lære norsk.

2 Jeg lærer meg norsk.

3 Jeg lærer ham norsk.

c I want to learn Norwegian.

1 Jeg har lyst til å lære norsk.

2 Jeg lærer meg norsk.

3 Jeg lærer ham norsk.

Language discovery 1

1 NEGATIVE SENTENCES

The negative in Norwegian is created by using **ikke**:

Jeg snakker *ikke* fransk.	*I don't speak French.*
Jeg har *ikke* lyst til å lære meg hindi.	*I don't want to learn Hindi.*
Studerer du *ikke* språk?	*Don't you study languages?*
Kommer du *ikke* fra Liverpool?	*Don't you come from Liverpool?*
Hvorfor jobber du *ikke*?	*Why don't you work?*
Nå bor hun *ikke* i Tokyo.	*She doesn't live in Tokyo now.*

LANGUAGE TIP

We usually say that **ikke** is placed in the third position in a sentence. In *wh-* questions we do not count the *wh-* word and still place **ikke** in the third position.

2 WANTING (TO DO) SOMETHING

As you saw in the last dialogue, when you want to do something you use the expression **å ha lyst til å gjøre noe**, while if you want something you have to use the expression **å ha lyst på noe**, as in the following examples:

Jeg *har lyst til å lære* meg hindi.	*I want to learn Hindi.*
Vi *har lyst på* indisk.	*We want (some) Indian food.*
Hun *har ikke lyst til å lære* seg japansk.	*She does not want to learn Japanese.*
Han *har ikke lyst på* indisk.	*He does not want (any) Indian food.*

1 Change the following sentences into negative ones, as in the example.

Jeg bor i Oslo. → Jeg bor ikke i Oslo.

- **a** Guro snakker kinesisk.
- **b** Kommer dere fra USA?
- **c** Du har lyst på kake.
- **d** Han kommer fra Frankrike.
- **e** Hvorfor er du trøtt?
- **f** Har du lyst til å gå tur?

2 Match the Norwegian with the English translation.

- **a** Jeg har lyst til å lære meg spansk.
- **b** Vi har lyst på pizza.
- **c** Hun har ikke lyst til å lære seg kinesisk.
- **d** Han har ikke lyst på fisk.

1. Don't you come from Finland?
2. He does not want to eat fish.
3. I want to learn Spanish.
4. We would like some pizza.

e	Kommer du ikke fra Finland?	**5**	She does not live in Russia now.
f	Hvorfor spiser du ikke?	**6**	She does not want to learn Chinese.
g	Nå bor hun ikke i Russland.	**7**	Why aren't you eating?
h	Hvorfor har du ikke lyst til å gå på tur?	**8**	They don't live in France now.
i	De bor ikke i Frankrike nå.	**9**	Why are you learning Norwegian?
j	Hvorfor lærer du deg norsk?	**10**	Why don't you want to take a walk?

Dialogue 2

02.03 *After having explained how negative sentences work, the teacher tells her students to work in groups and practice with one another. Listen carefully to the dialogue before answering the questions.*

1 When is Maggie going to Norway?

Lærer	Ok, nå jobber dere i grupper og snakker om ting dere gjør og ikke gjør. Husk å få ikke på riktig plass.
Audrey	Patrick, bor du i Spania?
Patrick	Nei, jeg bor ikke i Spania, jeg bor i England. David bor i Spania.
Sebastian	Wendy, snakker Isabel kinesisk?
Wendy	Ja, det gjør hun. Og hun snakker også fransk.
Heath	Gordon, har du en hund?
Gordon	Ja, det har jeg.
Richard	Ruth, kjenner du Anthony?
Ruth	Nei, jeg gjør ikke det.
Cathleen	Når drar du til Norge, Maggie?
Maggie	Jeg drar ikke til Norge.
Cathleen	Hvorfor ikke?
Maggie	Fordi jeg har ikke tid.

2 Re-read the dialogue and answer these questions.

- **a** Who speaks Chinese?
- **b** Who lives in Spain?
- **c** Who owns a dog?
- **d** Who does not know Anthony?
- **e** Why isn't Maggie going to Norway?

Language discovery 2

1 ANSWERING (NEGATIVE) QUESTIONS

As you can see from the last dialogue, when you are asked a yes / no question you have several ways to answer. This also depends on whether or not the question is negative. Look at these examples and note the differences, then answer the questions.

Bor du i Spania?	*Do you live in Spain?*
Ja, jeg bor i Spania.	*Yes, I live in Spain.*
Nei, jeg bor ikke i Spania.	*No, I don't live in Spain.*
Bor du ikke i Spania?	*Don't you live in Spain?*
Jo, jeg bor i Spania.	*Yes, I live in Spain.*
Nei, jeg bor ikke i Spania.	*No, I don't live in Spain.*

1 What words do we use to say *yes* in Norwegian?

2 What word do we use to say *no* in Norwegian?

3 Choose the right positive answer to the following questions.

- **a** Bor han i Stavanger?
  - **1** Ja, han bor i Stavanger.
  - **2** Jo, han bor i Stavanger.
- **b** Bor han ikke i Stavanger?
  - **1** Jo, han bor i Stavanger.
  - **2** Ja, han bor i Stavanger.
- **c** Kommer du fra Norge?
  - **1** Ja, jeg kommer fra Norge.
  - **2** Jo, jeg kommer fra Norge.
- **d** Kommer du ikke fra Norge?
  - **1** Ja, jeg kommer fra Norge.
  - **2** Jo, jeg kommer fra Norge.

2 SHORT ANSWERS

Like in the English language, short answers can also be given to questions in Norwegian, as you can see in the following examples:

Liker du fisk?	*Do you like fish?*
Ja, det gjør jeg.	*Yes, I do.*
Nei, jeg gjør ikke det.	*No, I don't.*
Liker du ikke fisk?	*Don't you like fish?*
Jo, det gjør jeg.	*Yes, I do.*
Nei, jeg gjør ikke det.	*No, I don't.*

4 Translate the answers to the following questions.

a Snakker du norsk? — *Do you speak Norwegian?*
   1 Ja, det gjør jeg. ________________
   2 Nei, jeg gjør ikke det. ________________

b Har du en hund? — *Do you have a dog?*
   1 Ja, det har jeg. ________________
   2 Nei, jeg har det ikke. ________________

c Er hun norsk? — *Is she Norwegian?*
   1 Ja, det er hun. ________________
   2 Nei, hun er det ikke. ________________

5 Complete the following answers. You can also use the translations for help.

a Snakker han ikke engelsk? — *Doesn't he speak English?*
   1 Jo, ________________. — *Yes, he does.*
   2 Nei, ________________. — *No, he doesn't.*

b Har hun ikke en katt? — *Doesn't she have a cat?*
   1 Jo, ________________. — *Yes, she does.*
   2 Nei, ________________. — *No, she doesn't.*

c Er han ikke gammel? — *Is he not old?*
   1 Jo, ________________. — *Yes, he is.*
   2 Nei, ________________. — *No, he is not.*

Practice

1 02.04 **Listen carefully to the following summary and then read it out loud. Try to imitate the Norwegian pronunciation.**

Peder og Jonas bor i Bergen, men Peder kommer ikke fra Bergen, han kommer fra Kristiansand. Amanda kommer fra USA, men nå bor hun i Bergen, fordi hun studerer ved Universitetet. Amanda og Peder er venner, men Amanda kjenner ikke Jonas. Amanda har en venninne som heter Harriet og kommer fra Skottland. Hun studerer språk og snakker engelsk, norsk, fransk og spansk, men de andre snakker bare engelsk og norsk.

2 **Re-read the summary and answer these questions.**

a Where does Peder come from?
b Where does Amanda come from?
c Where do they live?
d Why is Amanda in Norway?
e What does Harriet study?
f What languages do Peder, Jonas and Amanda speak?
g What languages does Harriet speak?

3 **Write a paragraph in which you talk about what you do (not do) or have and what languages you do (not) speak or study.**

____

____

____

____

Test yourself

1 Change the following sentences into negative ones, as in the example.

Jeg bor i Oslo. → Jeg bor ikke i Oslo.

a Hun snakker spansk.
b Har du lyst på pizza?
c Han lærer seg tysk.
d Jeg kommer fra England.
e Har dere lyst til å lære dere fransk?
f Snakker du norsk?
g Kommer du fra Australia?
h Han snakker arabisk.
i De drar til Norge.
j Han heter Walid.

2 Rearrange the words into sentences. Don't forget to place the capital letter on the first word.

a	Oslo	jeg	nå	ikke	bor	i	.
b	ikke	du	Bergen	bor	i	?	
c	du	kommer	hvorfor	ikke	?		
d	USA	ikke	kommer	han	fra	.	
e	to	har	ikke	jeg	katter	.	

3 Write a short summary of the first dialogue.

____
____
____
____

4 Answer the following questions with information about yourself.

a Hva heter du?
b Hvor kommer du fra?
c Hvor bor du?
d Hvilke språk snakker du?
e Hva gjør du nå?
f Hva har du lyst til å gjøre?
g Hva har du lyst på?

SELF CHECK

	I CAN ...
○	... ask and answer (negative) questions.
○	... say what languages I do (not) speak.
○	... say what I want and do not want to do.
○	... talk about what I am doing now.

3

In this unit, you will learn how to:

» count from 0 to 1,000,000,000.

» say how old you are.

» use singular and plural nouns in *a* and *the* forms.

» use some common prepositions of place.

Hvor mange bøker har du?

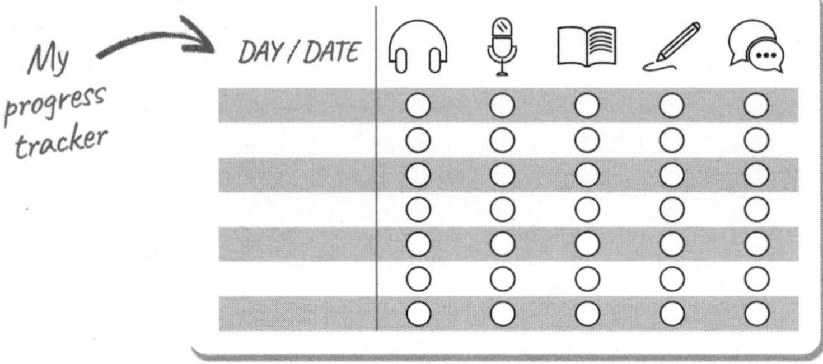

Numbers

Å telle (*to count*) in Norwegian is not that difficult, once you learn a thing or two. Since Norwegian has three genders, **nummer** (*the number*) **one** can be **én**, **ei** or **ett**, according to which **kjønn** (*gender*) the following **entall** (*singular*) **substantiv** (*noun*) is. However, this happens only for number one, since all other numbers are **flertall** (*plural*) and the plural form is the same for all genders. As with English, Norwegian numbers from 1 to 20 have a specific name, and so do all other tens, while from 21 to 29 (and from 31 to 39, etc.) we only have to add the unit: 21 is **tjueen** (*20 + one*).

Can you work out what the numbers 45, 67 and 82 are?

Vocabulary builder

03.01 Listen to the following numbers, and then repeat, trying to imitate the Norwegian pronunciation.

NUMBERS		NUMBERS	
null	*0*	tretti	*30*
én / ei / ett	*1*	førti	*40*
to	*2*	femti	*50*
tre	*3*	seksti	*60*
fire	*4*	sytti	*70*
fem	*5*	åtti	*80*
seks	*6*	nitti	*90*
sju / syv	*7*	(ett) hundre	*100*
åtte	*8*	(ett) hundre og en	*101*
ni	*9*	to hundre	*200*
ti	*10*	tre hundre	*300*
elleve	*11*	fire hundre og femtiseks	*456*
tolv	*12*	(ett) tusen	*1,000*
tretten	*13*	sju / syv tusen	*7,000*
fjorten	*14*	ti tusen	*10,000*
femten	*15*	(ett) hundre tusen	*100,000*
seksten	*16*	en million	*1,000,000*
sytten	*17*	en milliard	*1,000,000,000*
atten	*18*		
nitten	*19*		
tjue	*20*		
tjueen	*21*		

LANGUAGE TIP

There are still many people who count in the old way, where 21 is **én og tyve** (*lit. one and 20*), etc. This is similar to the Danish way of counting. In some areas of Norway, it is very common to encounter people working in shops who still do this, so sometimes you may have to think twice about the amount you need to pay!

1 Read out loud the numbers in the following examples. Where does the og (*and*) always come?

576 **fem hundre og syttiseks**

5,795 **fem tusen sju hundre og nittifem**

10,010 **ti tusen og ti**

3,005 **tre tusen og fem**

2 Write the following numbers as words and then read them out loud.

a 56 ____________________

b 89 ____________________

c 97 ____________________

d 74 ____________________

e 25 ____________________

f 33 ____________________

g 110 ____________________

h 563 ____________________

i 6,897 ____________________

j 10,345 ____________________

k 40,567 ____________________

l 357,500 ____________________

NEW EXPRESSIONS

Some of these new expressions are used in the following dialogues. Note their meaning and the differences between the various alternatives.

Hvor mange språk snakker du?	*How many languages do you speak?*
Jeg snakker sju språk.	*I speak seven languages.*
Hvor mye te drikker du?	*How much tea do you drink?*
Jeg drikker mye te.	*I drink a lot of tea.*
Hvor mange barn har du?	*How many children do you have?*
Jeg har fem barn.	*I have five children.*
Hvor gammel er du?	*How old are you?*
Jeg er tjue år gammel.	*I'm 20 years old.*
Jeg er tjue år.	*I'm 20 years (old).*
Jeg er tjue.	*I'm 20.*
Jeg har det travelt.	*I'm in a hurry.*
Det er lenge siden sist.	*Long time no see.*

Dialogue 1

03.02 *Daniel meets Amalie at the metro station after not seeing her for a long time and they catch up. Listen carefully to the dialogue before answering the questions.*

1 What does Daniel suggest they do?

Amalie	Hei Daniel, takk for sist!
Daniel	Hei! Det er lenge siden sist, hvordan har du det?
Amalie	Jeg har det bra, takk, hva med deg?
Daniel	Jeg har det også bra. Hva gjør du for tiden?
Amalie	Jeg jobber ved universitetet, jeg er lærer.
Daniel	Så flott, gratulerer!
Amalie	Takk, hva gjør du?
Daniel	Jeg jobber i banken. Bor du fortsatt på Tøyen?
Amalie	Nei, jeg bor på Frogner nå. Hva med deg?
Daniel	Jeg bor på Vinderen, men jeg vil gjerne flytte til Grünerløkka.
Amalie	Ja, det er fint der, men er det ikke mye bråk i helgene?
Daniel	Ja, det er nok det, men jeg er ofte på hytta da, så det er ikke et problem.
Amalie	Jeg skjønner. Det er bra.
Daniel	Har du lyst på noe å drikke? Vi kan sitte på kafé og snakke litt mer.
Amalie	Ja, hvorfor ikke? Jeg har det ikke travelt.
Daniel	Så bra! Da går vi.

2 Read the dialogue again and answer the questions.

a Where did Amalie live before?
b Where does she live now?
c Where does Daniel live?
d Where does Amalie work?
e Where does Daniel work?

3 Look at the dialogue again, then match the Norwegian with the English translation.

a Så flott, gratulerer!
b Hva gjør du for tiden?
c Jeg har det ikke travelt.
d Det er ikke et problem.

1 I'm not in a hurry.
2 That's great, congratulations!
3 It's not a problem.
4 What are you doing at the moment?

4 How do Amalie and Daniel say the following?

a I see.

1 Hva med deg?

2 Jeg skjønner.

3 Hvorfor ikke?

b How about you?

1 Hva med deg?

2 Jeg skjønner.

3 Hvorfor ikke?

c Why not?

1 Hva med deg?

2 Jeg skjønner.

3 Hvorfor ikke?

Language discovery 1

PREPOSITIONS OF PLACE

In Norwegian there are many prepositions. Here we are going to focus on two prepositions of place which are very common and can be used in a number of different situations. Look at the following table and try to memorize the differences.

<table>
<tr><th>PÅ</th><th>English</th><th>I</th><th>English</th></tr>
<tr><td colspan="2">På can be used to mean on:</td><td colspan="2">I can be used to mean in(side):</td></tr>
<tr><td>Katten er på skapet.
Flaska er på bordet.</td><td>The cat is on the cupboard.
The bottle is on the table.</td><td>Katten er i skapet.
Flaska er i kjøleskapet.</td><td>The cat is in the cupboard.
The bottle is in the fridge.</td></tr>
<tr><td colspan="2">På is also used when you say that you live in a small town (one that has fewer than 8,000 inhabitants):</td><td colspan="2">I is used when you say that you live in a (big) city:</td></tr>
<tr><td>Jeg bor på Portree.
Jeg bor på Løken.</td><td>I live in Portree.
I live in Løken.</td><td>Jeg bor i New York.
Jeg bor i Oslo.</td><td>I live in New York.
I live in Oslo.</td></tr>
<tr><td colspan="2">På is also used when you live on an island (even if it is as big as Iceland):</td><td colspan="2">I is used when you want to say in which country you live (unless it is an island):</td></tr>
<tr><td>Jeg bor på Skye.
Jeg bor på Island.</td><td>I live in Skye.
I live in Iceland.</td><td>Jeg bor i USA.
Jeg bor i Norge.</td><td>I live in the USA.
I live in Norway.</td></tr>
</table>

When you want to say in which area of a town / city you live, or are, you have to use **på**:		When you want to say in which street, avenue, etc. you live, or are, you have to use **i**:	
Jeg bor på Notting Hill.	*I live in Notting Hill.*	**Jeg bor i Oxford Street.**	*I live in Oxford Street.*
To say that you are in some places, like cafés and schools, you use **på**:		While in other places you use **i**:	
De er på kafé. **Jeg er på skolen.**	*They are at the café.* *I am at school.*	**Jeg jobber i banken.** **Jeg er i butikken.**	*I work in a bank.* *I am in the shop.*
With the majority of means of transport you use **på**:		But with some modes of transport you also use **i**:	
Jeg er på trikken. **Jeg er på bussen.** **Jeg er på T-banen.** **Jeg er på toget.** **Jeg er på flyet.** **Jeg er på sykkelen.**	*I am on the tram.* *I am on the bus.* *I am on the metro.* *I am on the train.* *I am on the plane.* *I am on the bike.*	**Jeg er i bilen.** **Jeg er i båten.**	*I am in the car.* *I am on the boat.*

1 Fill in the blanks with the right preposition. (Pay attention: some of the sentences need a different preposition to i or på!)

a Sven og jeg studerer _______________ Oslo.
b Kommer du _______________ Bergen?
c Jeg bor også _______________ Glasgow.
d Vi bor _______________ Norge.
e Hotellet ligger _______________ Karl Johans gate.
f Du kommer _______________ London.
g Boka ligger _______________ hylla.
h Melken er _______________ kjøleskapet.
i Gloria jobber _______________ skolen.
j Han er _______________ trikken.
k Dere er _______________ kafé.

Dialogue 2

03.03 *Kristine is in a bookshop and she is looking for a book to give her friend, who loves reading. She is uncertain, and she asks the bookseller for advice. Listen carefully to the dialogue before answering the questions.*

1 Why is it difficult to find a suitable book?

2 Where does she go in the end?

Bokhandleren	Hei, kan jeg hjelpe deg?
Kristine	Ja, takk, jeg leter etter ei bok til en venn, men jeg vet ikke helt hva jeg skal kjøpe, han leser mye.
Bokhandleren	Hva er han interessert i?
Kristine	Han er interessert i mange ting, og jeg vil gjerne finne noe spennende.
Bokhandleren	Kanskje en roman? Liker han krim?
Kristine	Já, men han leser ofte krim, så jeg vet ikke hva han har fra før.
Bokhandleren	Jeg skjønner.
Kristine	Kanskje noe om reiser, han liker å reise.
Bokhandleren	Ja, reisebøkene ligger i andre etasje, ved siden av ordbøker.
Kristine	Tusen takk, jeg skal ta en titt.
Bokhandleren	Bare hyggelig.

3 Read the dialogue again and answer the questions.

a What is Kristine's friend interested in?
b What does Kristine's friend like doing?
c Where are the travel books?

4 Read the dialogue again, then match the Norwegian with the English translation.

a Han leser mye.
b Hva er han interessert i?
c Jeg vil gjerne finne noe spennende.
d Jeg skal ta en titt.
e Bare hyggelig.

1 I'm going to take a look.
2 You're welcome.
3 He reads a lot.
4 What is he interested in?
5 I would like to find something exciting.

5 How does Kristine say the following?

a many things
1 mange ting
2 noe
3 jeg skjønner
4 kanskje

b maybe
1 jeg skjønner
2 kanskje
3 før
4 ved siden av

c something

1 mange ting
2 noe
3 jeg skjønner
4 kanskje

d next to

1 mange ting
2 noe
3 før
4 ved siden av

e I see

1 jeg skjønner
2 kanskje
3 før
4 ved siden av

f before

1 mange ting
2 noe
3 før
4 ved siden av

Language discovery 2

1 SINGULAR AND PLURAL NOUNS, DEFINITE AND INDEFINITE FORMS

Norwegian has three genders: masculine, feminine and neuter. We can recognize the gender of the noun by looking at the singular forms of all three genders. It becomes less easy to recognize the gender from the indefinite plural forms, and it is impossible to tell by looking at the definite plural.

Masculine

Norwegian indefinite singular masculine nouns take the article **en** (*a / an*) before the noun:

***en* bil**	*a car*
***en* dag**	*a day*
***en* gutt**	*a boy*
***en* katt**	*a cat*
***en* venn**	*a friend*
***en* pizza**	*a pizza*
***en* lærer**	*a teacher*
***en* mann**	*a man*

In the <u>definite singular form</u>, the article **en** becomes the end of the noun:

1 Complete the following nouns with the definite ending.

- **a** bil___ *the car*
- **b** dag___ *the day*
- **c** gutt___ *the boy*
- **d** katt___ *the cat*
- **e** venn___ *the friend*
- **f** pizza___ *the pizza*
- **g** lærer___ *the teacher*
- **h** mann___ *the man*

In the <u>indefinite plural form</u>, most of the nouns change their ending to **-er**:

2 Complete the following nouns with the indefinite plural ending.

- **a** bil___ *some cars*
- **b** dag___ *some days*
- **c** gutt___ *some boys*
- **d** katt___ *some cats*
- **e** venn___ *some friends*
- **f** pizza___ *some pizzas*
- **g** lærere *some teachers*
- **h** menn *some men*
- **i** What happens to *teachers* and *men*?

In the <u>definite plural form</u>, the nouns change their ending to **-ene (-ne)**:

3 Complete the following nouns with the definite plural ending.

- **a** bil___ *the cars*
- **b** dag___ *the days*
- **c** gutt___ *the boys*
- **d** katt___ *the cats*
- **e** venn___ *the friends*
- **f** pizza___ *the pizzas*
- **g** lærerne *the teachers*
- **h** menn___ *the men*
- **i** What happens to *teachers*?

Feminine

Norwegian <u>indefinite singular feminine nouns</u> take the article **ei** (*a / an*) before the noun:

***ei* dame**	*a woman*
***ei* jente**	*a girl*

***ei* kake** *a cake*
***ei* lampe** *a lamp*
***ei* skive** *a slice*
***ei* venninne** *a (female) friend*
***ei* bok** *a book*
***ei* natt** *a night*

In the definite singular feminine form, we add an **-a** at the end of the noun:

4 Complete the following nouns with the definite ending.

- **a** dam___ *the woman*
- **b** jent___ *the girl*
- **c** kak___ *the cake*
- **d** lamp___ *the lamp*
- **e** skiv___ *the slice*
- **f** venninn___ *the (female) friend*
- **g** bok___ *the book*
- **h** natt___ *the night*

In the indefinite plural form, most of the nouns change their ending to **-er**, but some also change a vowel at the same time:

5 Complete the following nouns with the indefinite plural ending.

- **a** dam___ *some women*
- **b** jent___ *some girls*
- **c** kak___ *some cakes*
- **d** lamp___ *some lamps*
- **e** skiv___ *some slices*
- **f** venninn___ *some (female) friends*
- **g** bøk___ *some books*
- **h** nett___ *some nights*
- **i** What happens to *books* and *nights*?

In the definite plural form, the nouns change their ending to **-ene**:

6 Complete the following nouns with the definite plural ending.

- **a** dam___ *the women*
- **b** jent___ *the girls*
- **c** kak___ *the cakes*
- **d** lamp___ *the lamps*
- **e** skiv___ *the slices*
- **f** venninn___ *the (female) friends*
- **g** bøk___ *the books*
- **h** nett___ *the nights*
- **i** What happens to *books* and *nights*?

LANGUAGE TIP

Norwegians who speak 'conservative' **bokmål** do not use the feminine, so all feminine nouns can also be masculine. An example of this is the word **kvinne** (*woman*), which is often used with the masculine article **en**, even if it is clearly feminine.

***en* kvinne**	*a woman*	***ei* kvinne**	*a woman*
kvinne*n*	*the woman*	**kvinn*a***	*the woman*
kvinner	*some women*	**kvinner**	*some women*
kvinne*ne*	*the women*	**kvinne*ne***	*the women*

Neuter

Norwegian indefinite singular neuter nouns take the article **et** (*a / an*) before the noun:

***et* eple**	*an apple*
***et* hotell**	*a hotel*
***et* vindu**	*a window*
***et* bord**	*a table*
***et* brød**	*a loaf of bread*
***et* hjem**	*a home*
***et* hus**	*a house*
***et* kurs**	*a course*
***et* rom**	*a room*
***et* skap**	*a cabinet / closet / cupboard*

In the definite singular form, the article **et** becomes the end of the noun:

7 Complete the following nouns with the definite ending.

- **a** epl_______ — *the apple*
- **b** hotell_______ — *the hotel*
- **c** vindu_______ — *the window*
- **d** bord_______ — *the table*
- **e** brød_______ — *the bread*
- **f** hjemm_______ — *the home*
- **g** hus_______ — *the house*
- **h** kurs_______ — *the course*
- **i** romm_______ — *the room*
- **j** skap_______ — *the cabinet / closet / cupboard*
- **k** What happens to *homes* and *rooms*?

In the <u>indefinite plural form</u>, the nouns that have more than one vowel change their ending to **-er**, while the nouns with only one vowel just lose the article of the base form and remain unchanged:

8 Complete the following nouns with the indefinite plural ending.

a epl______	*some apples*
b hotell______	*some hotels*
c vindu______	*some windows*
d bord	*some tables*
e brød	*some loaves of bread*
f hjem	*some homes*
g hus	*some houses*
h kurs	*some courses*
i rom	*some rooms*
j skap	*some cabinets / closets*

k What happens to the majority of the nouns?

In the <u>definite plural form</u>, the nouns change their ending to **-ene**:

9 Complete the following nouns with the definite plural ending.

a epl______	*the apples*
b hotell______	*the hotels*
c vindu______	*the windows*
d bord______	*the tables*
e brød______	*the loaves of bread*
f hjemm______	*the homes*
g hus ______	*the houses*
h kurs______	*the courses*
i romm______	*the rooms*
j skap______	*the cabinets / closets*

k What happens to *homes* and *rooms*?

2 COMPOUND WORDS, DEFINITE AND INDEFINITE FORMS

In Norwegian, it is very common to have compound words. The most important rule these words follow is that they always take the gender of the last noun of the compound. Therefore, if the last noun is neuter with only one vowel, they will not take any **-er** ending in the indefinite plural form.

10 With the help of the previous examples, find out the gender of the following compounds.

a Barnehage

1 en | 2 ei | 3 et

b Bokhylle

1 en | 2 ei | 3 et

c Brødskive

1 en | 2 ei | 3 et

d Kjøleskap

1 en | 2 ei | 3 et

11 Match the Norwegian with the English translations.

a barnehage	1 fridge
b bokhylle	2 slice of bread
c brødskive	3 bookshelf
d kjøleskap	4 kindergarten

Practice

1 Marte is a Norwegian student writing to her English friend Sebastian, who is learning Norwegian. Read her email and answer the questions.

New message

Kjære Sebastian,

Jeg heter Marte, er 14 år og bor i Ringsaker, en kommune på Hedmarken i Innlandet fylke i Norge. Jeg liker sport og naturen, og har mange kjæledyr hjemme. Jeg har tre hunder, to katter, og en hest. Jeg har også to undulater, de er en type papegøye som kommer fra Australia. Jeg bor på gård, så vi har også andre dyr, som sauer, kyr og geiter. Jeg vil gjerne ha en skilpadde også, men mamma sa jeg ikke får lov, dessverre.

Hva med deg? Hvor gammel er du? Hvor bor du? Har du noen dyr? Hva liker du å gjøre? Fortell meg alt!

Beste hilsen
Marte

a How many pets does Marte have?
b How many dogs does she have?
c How many cats?
d How many birds?
e How many horses?
f What is the animal that she would like but is not allowed to have?

2 How does Marte say the following?

a farm
- **1** jeg får ikke lov
- **2** gård
- **3** dessverre

b unfortunately
- **1** jeg får ikke lov
- **2** gård
- **3** dessverre

c I am not allowed
- **1** jeg får ikke lov
- **2** gård
- **3** dessverre

3 Write a short email like the one written by Marte. Feel free to invent, and use as many numbers and new words as possible.

____

____

____

____

____

____

Test yourself

1 Translate the following sentences.

a They eat a lot of bread.
b He is 34 years old.
c I am in a hurry.
d The books are in the closet.
e How old are you?
f She drinks a lot of coffee.
g The bottle is on the table.

2 Rearrange the words into sentences; don't forget to place the capital letter on the first word.

a	sju	snakker	jeg	språk	.	
b	travelt	har	jeg	det	.	
c	lenge	er	det	sist	siden	.
d	skapet	står	katten	på	.	
e	komme	du	kan	meg	til	?
f	deg	hjelpe	jeg	kan	?	
g	krim	han	liker	?		

3 Complete the following table:

Entall – *singular*		Flertall – *plural*		*English translation*
Ubestemt – *indeterminate*	Bestemt – *determinate*	Ubestemt – *indeterminate*	Bestemt – *determinate*	
_______ **barnehage**				
_______ **bokhylle**				
_______ **brødskive**				
_______ **kjøleskap**				
_______ **nattbord**				
_______ **pauserom**				
_______ **skrivebord**				
_______ **spedbarn**				
_______ **spisebord**				
_______ **spørsmål**				
_______ **spørsmålstegn**				

SELF CHECK

	I CAN ...
○	... handle numbers and quantities.
○	... say how old I am.
○	... use nouns correctly.
○	... use new prepositions.
○	... write an email to a friend.

Review 1

1 Hei! Hyggelig å treffe deg!

1 Match the Norwegian with the English.

a Jeg snakker med henne.
b Han snakker med meg.
c Vi snakker med dere.
d De snakker med meg.
e Du snakker med oss.
f Vi snakker med dem.

1 He talks to me.
2 We talk to them.
3 I talk to her.
4 We talk to you (*plural*).
5 You (*singular*) talk to us.
6 They talk to me.

2 Translate the following sentences into English.

a Har hun ei venninne?
b Hvem er du?
c Når kommer du?
d Hva gjør hun der?
e Hva studerer du?
f Hvor studerer du?

3 Translate the following sentences into Norwegian and say them out loud.

a Her name is Fatima.
b I live in Bergen, but I come from Stavanger.
c What is your name?
d Abby and Maja are friends.
e Sven is a student.
f Nora is a doctor.

4 Match the question with the correct answer.

a Hvordan har du det?
b Hva heter du?
c Hvor kommer du fra?
d Bor du i Oslo?
e Kommer du fra Norge?
f Når kommer du?

1 Jeg kommer snart.
2 Jeg har det bra, takk.
3 Ja, jeg kommer fra Trondheim.
4 Jeg heter Maja.
5 Jeg kommer fra England.
6 Nei, jeg bor i Bergen.

5 Complete the following crossword and find the hidden sentence.

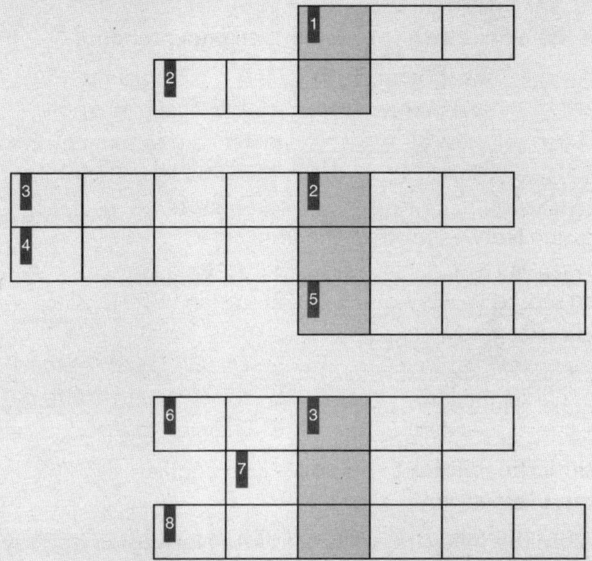

Across:

What is the Norwegian for the following?

1 hello
2 what
3 how
4 (to) come
5 thanks
6 (to) work
7 from
8 (to) speak

Down:

What is the Norwegian for the following?

1 (to) have
2 it
3 well / good

Have you found the hidden sentence? What does it mean?

____

2 Hvilket språk snakker du nå?

1 Fill in the blanks with the correct personal pronoun.

Hei, **a)** ________ heter Grete, og **b)** ________ kommer fra Norge. Og **c)** ________ heter Bernard og kommer fra Australia. **d)** ________ snakker ikke norsk, men **e)** ________ snakker engelsk sammen. Hva heter **f)** ________? **g)** ________ heter Maria og Javier, og **h)** ________ kommer fra Spania. Snakker **i)** ________ engelsk? Nei, **j)** ________ snakker bare norsk og spansk.

2 Translate the following sentences into English.

- **a** Hvilke språk snakker du?
- **b** Hvilket språk snakker du?
- **c** Kommer du ikke fra Bristol?
- **d** Jeg har lyst til å lære meg hindi.
- **e** Jo, han bor i Stavanger.
- **f** Nei, han gjør ikke det.
- **g** Hun studerer språk.

3 Translate the following sentences into Norwegian and say them out loud.

- **a** Aren't you Norwegian?
- **b** Do you live in Oslo?
- **c** I don't live in Bergen now.
- **d** I would like to watch a movie.
- **e** I would like some chocolate.
- **f** I speak English, Norwegian, Italian, French, German, Swedish and Danish.

4 Answer the following questions. In some cases you can also use short answers.

- **a** Hva heter du?
- **b** Hvor bor du?
- **c** Hvor kommer du fra?
- **d** Hvilke språk snakker du?
- **e** Hva gjør du nå?
- **f** Har du en hund?
- **g** Har du lyst på sjokolade?
- **h** Har du ikke lyst til å lære deg norsk?

5 Complete the following crossword and find the mystery word.

Across:

1 What language do people speak in Sweden?
2 What language do Norwegians speak?
3 What language do Russians speak?
4 What language do most people speak in the USA?
5 What language do Italians speak?

Down:

Have you found the mystery word? What is it? ________

3 Hvor mange bøker har du?

1 Fill in the blanks with the correct preposition.

a De sitter ________ kafé.
b Jeg går ________ skolen.
c Vi bor ________ Norge.
d Boka er ________ sekken.
e Jeg har lyst ________ å lære meg hindi.
f Kan du komme ________ meg?
g Du kommer ________ London.
h Sven og jeg studerer lingvistikk ________ universitetet.
i Hva snakker du ________ ?

2 Fill in the blanks with the number(s) in brackets.

a Maja har ________ katter og ________ hund. (2, 1)
b Jeg har ________ barn. (5)
c Hvor gammel er du? Jeg er ________ år gammel. (58)
d Hvor mange språk snakker du? Jeg snakker ________ språk. (7)
e Jeg har ________ bøker med meg i dag. (6)

3 Translate the following sentences into Norwegian and say them out loud.

- **a** How many languages do you speak?
- **b** How much bread do you eat?
- **c** I eat a lot of pizza.
- **d** How many children do you have?
- **e** I'm 20.
- **f** Long time no see.

4 Fill in the blanks with the correct form of the nouns in brackets.

- **a** Jeg spiser ________ . (eple)
- **b** ________ snakker bare norsk. (mann)
- **c** ________ er god. (kake)
- **d** Min ________ heter Pia. (venninne)
- **e** ________ ligger i ________ . (hus, by)
- **f** Jeg har lyst på ________ . (brød)
- **g** ________ sitter under ________ . (katt, bord)

5 Complete the following crossword.

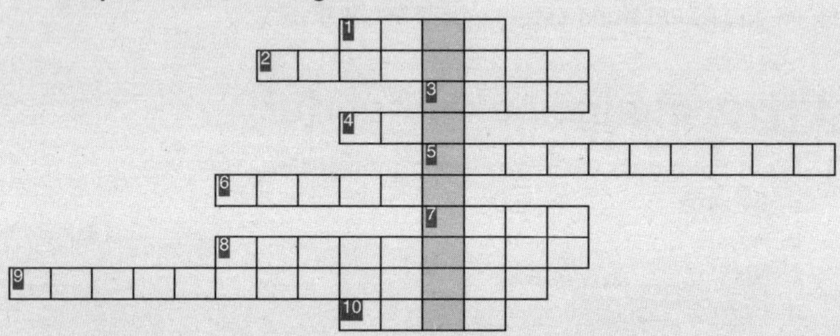

Across:

- **1** child
- **2** bookshelf
- **3** boy
- **4** day
- **5** writing desk
- **6** woman
- **7** cat
- **8** slice of bread
- **9** question mark
- **10** dog

Down:

Have you found the mystery word? What is it? What does it mean?

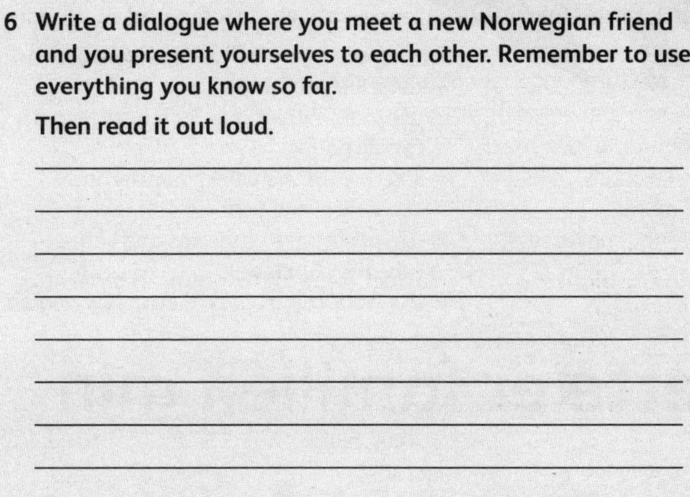

6 **Write a dialogue where you meet a new Norwegian friend and you present yourselves to each other. Remember to use everything you know so far.**

Then read it out loud.

4

In this unit, you will learn how to:

» describe your family.
» use indefinite and definite articles with family nouns.
» say days of the week, months and seasons of the year.
» use possessive pronouns and some adverbs of place.
» ask what things are called in Norwegian.

Dette er familien min

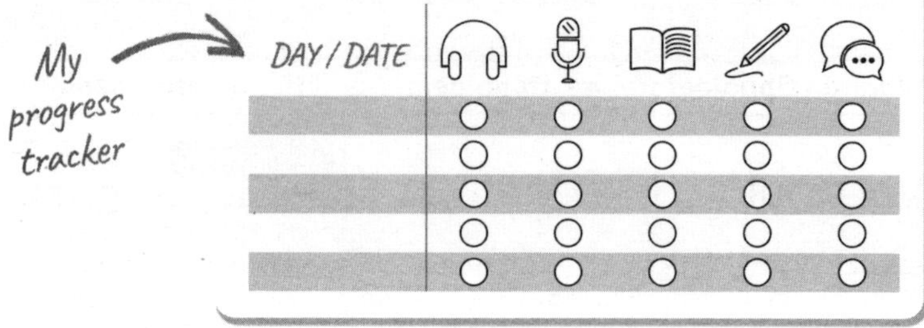

Family relations

In Norwegian, the words used to refer to one's **foreldre** (*parents*) can be **mamma** (*mum*) and **pappa** (*dad*), or **mor** (*mother*) and **far** (*father*). When people are **skilt** (*divorced*), they can also have a **bonusmamma** (*stepmother*) and a **bonuspappa** (*stepfather*). When talking about **besteforeldre** (*grandparents*) we can be very precise, as Norwegian not only has **bestemor** (*grandmother*) and **bestefar** (*grandfather*), but also specific words to refer to them: **mormor** (*the mother's mother*), **morfar** (*the mother's father*), **farmor** (*the father's mother*) and **farfar** (*the father's father*). When we talk about **søsken** (*siblings*), we have **søster** (*sister*) and **bror** (*brother*), **stesøster** (*stepsister*) and **stebror** (*stepbrother*). To talk about **barna** (*children*), or **bonusbarna** (*stepchildren*), we have **datter** (*daughter*), **stedatter** (*stepdaughter*), **sønn** (*son*), **stesønn** (*stepson*), and **barnebarn** (*grandchildren*), and **søskenbarn** (*cousins*) can be a **fetter** (*male cousin*) or a **kusine** (*female* *cousin*). Furthermore, a **tante** (*aunt*) and **onkel** (*uncle*) can have a **nevø** (*nephew*) or a **niese** (*niece*). When they are **gift** (*married*), a **mann** (*husband*) and **kone** (*wife*) usually have **svigerforeldre** (pl. *in-laws*), specifically a **svigermor** (*mother-in-law*) and a **svigerfar** (*father-in-law*), to which they are **svigersønn** (*son-in-law*) and **svigerdatter** (*daughter-in-law*). If they have siblings, they can also have a **svoger** (*brother-in-law*) or a **svigerinne** (*sister-in-law*), and if you are **enslig** you are *single*.

LANGUAGE/CULTURE TIP

Even though **stefar**, **stemor**, **stedatter**, **stesønn**, **stebarn** are not officially negative, many think that they have a slightly negative connotation, especially when referring directly to family members. Therefore, words such as **bonuspappa**, **bonusmamma**, **bonusdatter**, **bonussønn** and **bonusbarn** are used more and more frequently. Some people even skip the **ste-** and **bonus-** part altogether and just use **barn**, **søster**, **bror**, etc. even if they are talking about stepchildren or stepsiblings.

What do tippoldeforeldre, tippoldemor and tippoldefar mean?

Vocabulary builder

LANGUAGE TIP

In Norwegian, it is not necessary to begin months, days and seasons with a capital letter. Festivities such as Christmas and Easter (see Unit 9) do not require a capital letter either.

04.01 Listen to the following words, and then repeat, trying to imitate the Norwegian pronunciation.

DAYS OF THE WEEK

mandag	fredag	onsdag	søndag
tirsdag	lørdag	torsdag	

SEASONS

vinter	vår	sommer	høst
winter	*spring*	*summer*	*autumn*

MONTHS OF THE YEAR

januar	april	juli	oktober
februar	mai	august	november
mars	juni	september	desember

NEW EXPRESSIONS

Some of these new expressions are used in the following dialogues. Note their meanings and the differences between the various alternatives.

Hva betyr det?	*What does it mean?*
Nå forstår jeg!	*Now I understand!*
Hva heter «fiancé» på norsk?	*What's the Norwegian for 'fiancé'?*
Hva heter Toves forlovede?	*What is the name of Tove's fiancé?*
Hva mener du?	*What do you mean?*
Det er veldig vanskelig å huske alt.	*It's very difficult to remember everything.*
Åse og Martine er kusiner.	*Åse and Martine are cousins.*
Foreldrene mine kommer.	*My parents are coming.*
Min søster heter Astrid.	*My sister's name is Astrid.*
Farfar Arthur kommer med kona si.	*My grandfather is coming with his wife.*
Mammas søster heter Sigrid.	*My aunt's name is Sigrid. (lit. Mum's sister's name is Sigrid.)*
Det blir koselig.	*It's going to be cosy.*
Broren hans heter Ciarán.	*His brother's name is Ciarán.*
Søstera hans heter Siobhán.	*His sister's name is Siobhán.*

Dialogue 1

04.02 *Gwen is an exchange student in Norway. She and her friend Kenneth are at a party where she just met many new people. He helps her remember people's names and relationships to one another. Listen to the conversation and answer the questions.*

1 What does Gwen notice about the Norwegian words for *cousin***?**

Gwen	Hva heter hun som sitter der igjen? Og hvor gammel er hun?
Kenneth	Hun heter Solveig, er 25 år og er kjæresten til Morten.
Gwen	Kjæresten? Jeg forstår ikke, hva betyr det?
Kenneth	Kjæreste betyr «boyfriend», eller «girlfriend».
Gwen	Å, nå forstår jeg! Og hvem er han?
Kenneth	Han er Ola, han er 23, kommer fra Tromsø og er broren til Gudrun.
Gwen	Takk. Og han er ... hvordan sier man det? Hva heter «fiancé» på norsk?

Kenneth	Det heter «forlovede».
Gwen	Takk, hva heter Toves forlovede?
Kenneth	Han heter Johan, er 27 år gammel, og kommer fra Tønsberg.
Gwen	Takk. Det er veldig vanskelig å huske alt.
Kenneth	Ja, jeg vet det, men du er flink, og jeg kan hjelpe deg.
Gwen	Takk, du er snill! Hvem er hun som kommer hit?
Kenneth	Hun er Martine, kusina til Åse og Petter.
Gwen	Så Åse, Petter og Martine er søskenbarn, riktig?
Kenneth	Ja, det er helt riktig.
Gwen	Men hva er forskjellen mellom kusine og fetter da?
Kenneth	Åse og Martine er kusiner, for de er kvinner, men Petter er fetteren til Martine og Åse, for han er mann.
Gwen	Å ja! Så dere har tre forskjellige ord for «cousin».
Kenneth	Ja, det er sant.
Gwen	Jeg blir helt forvirret!

2 Re-read the dialogue and answer the following questions.

a Who are Solveig and Morten?
b Where do Gudrun and Ola come from?
c Who are they?
d Who is Tove?
e Who are Petter, Åse and Martine?

3 Look at the conversation again, then match the Norwegian with the English translation.

a Jeg forstår ikke, hva betyr det?
b Hvordan sier man det?
c Det er veldig vanskelig å huske alt.
d Hva heter hun igjen?
e Hvem er hun?
f Hva er forskjellen mellom kusine og fetter?

1 What's the difference between *kusine* and *fetter*?
2 Who is she?
3 How do you say that?
4 It's very difficult to remember everything.
5 I don't understand, what does it mean?
6 What's her name again?

4 How do Kenneth and Gwen say the following?

a difference

1 vanskelig **2** forskjellen **3** forvirret **4** riktig

b kind

1 snill **2** forvirret **3** riktig **4** kjæreste

c right

1 snill **2** vanskelig **3** riktig **4** kjæreste

d fiancé

1 forskjellen **2** forvirret **3** forlovede **4** kjæreste

e boyfriend / girlfriend

1 forskjellen **2** forvirret **3** forlovede **4** kjæreste

f difficult

1 vanskelig **2** forskjellen **3** forvirret **4** forlovede

Language discovery 1

1 SINGULAR AND PLURAL FAMILY NOUNS, DEFINITE AND INDEFINITE FORMS

Many of the words related to family tend to behave differently from other nouns, especially in the plural indefinite form.

Masculine

Norwegian indefinite singular masculine nouns take the article **en** (*a / an*) before the noun:

***en* bror** *a brother*
***en* far** *a father*
***en* fetter** *a (male) cousin*
***en* forelder** *a parent*
***en* nevø** *a nephew*
***en* onkel** *an uncle*
***en* svoger** *a brother-in-law*
***en* sønn** *a son*

In the definite singular form, the article **en** becomes the end of the noun:

1 Complete the following nouns with the definite ending.

a bror________	*the brother*
b far________	*the father*
c fetter________	*the (male) cousin*
d forelder________	*the parent*
e nevø________	*the nephew*
f onkel________	*the uncle*
g svoger________	*the brother-in-law*
h sønn________	*the son*

In the indefinite plural form, most of the nouns change their ending to **-er**, but some change their ending to **-re**:

2 Complete the following nouns with the indefinite plural ending.

a brød________	*some brothers*
b fed________	*some fathers*
c fette________	*some (male) cousins*
d foreld________	*some parents*
e nevø________	*some nephews*
f onkl________	*some uncles*
g svoge________	*some brothers-in-law*
h sønn________	*some sons*

In the definite plural form, the nouns change their ending to **-ene / -ne**, taking the base form from the indefinite plural:

3 Complete the following nouns with the definite plural ending.

a brødr________	*the brothers*
b fedr________	*the fathers*
c fetter________	*the (male) cousins*
d foreldr________	*the parents*
e nevø________	*the nephews*
f onkl________	*the uncles*
g svoger________	*the brothers-in-law*
h sønn________	*the sons*

Feminine

Norwegian indefinite singular feminine nouns take the article **ei** (*a / an*) before the noun:

***ei* datter**	*a daughter*
***ei* kone**	*a wife*

***ei* kusine** *a (female) cousin*
***ei* mor** *a mother*
***ei* niese** *a niece*
***ei* svigerinne** *a sister-in-law*
***ei* søster** *a sister*
***ei* tante** *an aunt*

In the definite singular feminine form, we add an **-a** at the end of the noun:

4 Complete the following nouns with the definite ending.

a datter________ *the daughter*
b kon________ *the wife*
c kusin________ *the (female) cousin*
d mor________ *the mother*
e nies________ *the niece*
f svigerinn________ *the sister-in-law*
g søster________ *the sister*
h tant________ *the aunt*

In the indefinite plural form, most of the nouns change their ending to **-re**, some change to **-er**, and some also change a vowel at the same time:

5 Complete the following nouns with the indefinite plural ending.

a døt________ *some daughters*
b kon________ *some wives*
c kusin________ *some (female) cousins*
d mød________ *some mothers*
e nies________ *some nieces*
f svigerinn________ *some sisters-in-law*
g søst________ *some sisters*
h tant________ *some aunts*
i What happens to *daughters* and *mothers*?

In the definite plural form, the nouns change their ending to **-ene**, taking the base form from the indefinite plural:

6 Complete the following nouns with the definite plural ending.

a døtr________ *the daughters*
b kon________ *the wives*
c kusin________ *the (female) cousins*
d mødr________ *the mothers*
e nies________ *the nieces*

f svigerinn_______ *the sisters-in-law*
g søstr_______ *the sisters*
h tant_______ *the aunts*
i What happens to *daughters* and *mothers*?

Neuter

Norwegian indefinite singular neuter nouns take the article **et** (*a / an*) before the noun:

***et* barn**	*a child*
***et* barnebarn**	*a grandchild*
***et* søsken**	*a sibling*
***et* søskenbarn**	*a cousin*

In the definite singular form, the article **et** becomes the end of the noun:

7 Complete the following nouns with the definite ending.

a barn_______ *the child*
b barnebarn_______ *the grandchild*
c søsken_______ *the sibling*
d søskenbarn_______ *the cousin*
e bonusbarn_______ *the stepchild*

In the indefinite plural form, the nouns that have more than one vowel change their ending to **-er** (**søsken** being an exception), while the ones with only one vowel, and the compounds made from those, just lose the article of the base form and remain unchanged:

8 Complete the following nouns with the indefinite plural ending. What happens to them?

a _______ *some children*
b _______ *some grandchildren*
c _______ *some siblings*
d _______ *some cousins*

In the definite plural form, some nouns change their ending to **-ene**, and some change to **-a**, taking the base form from the indefinite plural:

9 Complete the following nouns with the definite plural ending.

a barn_______ *the children*
b barnebarn_______ *the grandchildren*
c søskn_______ *the siblings*
d søskenbarn_______ *the cousins*
e What happens to *the siblings*?

LANGUAGE TIP

The word **barn** (*child*) is neuter, and is also one of the very few exceptions to the plural **-ene** ending, since it takes an **-a** at the end of the definite plural form:

et barn	*a child*	**barn**	*some children*
barnet	*the child*	**barna**	*the children*

10 Translate the following sentences into Norwegian and say them out loud.

- **a** The girls are playing.
- **b** The children are sleeping.
- **c** She has a child.
- **d** The mother is singing.
- **e** The fathers are talking.
- **f** This is my grandmother.
- **g** I have an uncle and an aunt.
- **h** They have three stepchildren.

2 SOME POSSESSIVE FORMS

As in English, Norwegian adds an **-s** at the end of the owner's name to indicate possession, but the apostrophe, and in this case not the **-s**, is only used when the owner's name already ends in **-s**.

Tims forlovede heter Frank.	*Tim's fiancé is Frank.*
Martines bil er blå.	*Martine's car is blue.*
Lars' stesønn heter Daniel.	*Lars' stepson is Daniel.*

Another way to say that something belongs to someone, or that someone is related to someone else, is by using the preposition **til**, as in the following examples:

Hun er dattera *til* Marte.	*She is Marte's daughter.*
Denne er boka *til* Marius.	*This is Marius' book.*

11 Fill in the blanks with the noun in the right form.

- **a** Khadijas ________ heter Wadan. (*brother*)
- **b** Väinös ________ er blå. (*house*)
- **c** Lars' ________ heter Daniel. (*stepson*)
- **d** Hun er ________ til Marte. (*daughter*)
- **e** Den er ________ til Szymon. (*dog*)

12 Match the Norwegian with the English translation.

- **a** Denne er min bok.
- **b** Du er stesøstera til Akram.
- **c** Bilen til Ulf er svart.
- **d** Denne boka er min.
- **e** Påls kjæreste heter Karl.
- **f** Han er Jons fetter.

1. Pål's boyfriend is Karl.
2. Ulf's car is black.
3. He is Jon's cousin.
4. You are Akram's stepsister.
5. This is my book.
6. This book is mine.

3 SOME ADVERBS OF PLACE

In Norwegian *here* is either **her** or **hit**, and *there* is either **der** or **dit**. **Hit** and **dit** indicate motion, while **her** and **der** indicate a static condition; there is no movement.

Jeg er *her*.	*I am here.*
Jeg kommer *hit*.	*I come here.*
Du er *der*.	*You are there.*
Du går *dit*.	*You go there.*

13 Fill in the blanks with the correct adverb of place.

- **a** Kan du komme ________? (*here*)
- **b** Hva heter hun som sitter ________ igjen? (*there*)
- **c** Hva gjør du ________? (*here*)
- **d** Når drar du ________? (*there*)
- **e** Dere kommer ________ i morgen. (*here*)
- **f** Han står ________ og venter. (*there*)
- **g** Vi ligger ________ og soler oss. (*here*)
- **h** Kan du gå ________ og se om hun kommer? (*there*)

Dialogue 2

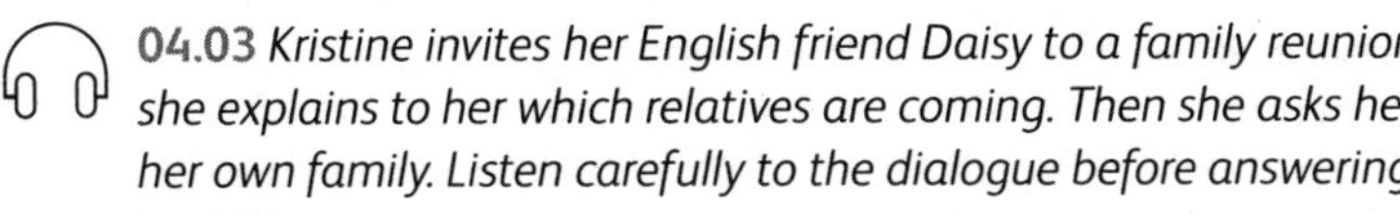

04.03 *Kristine invites her English friend Daisy to a family reunion, and she explains to her which relatives are coming. Then she asks her about her own family. Listen carefully to the dialogue before answering the questions.*

1 How many siblings does Kristine have?

Kristine	Foreldrene mine kommer, de heter Arne og Inger, og så søsknene mine: min søster, Astrid, er 23 år gammel og broren min Espen er 29, og er gift med Siri, hun er også 29, og de har et barn på 2 år, hun heter Camilla.
Daisy	Så Siri er din svigerinne, riktig?

Kristine	Ja, akkurat. Morfar Magnus og mormor Guro kommer også, og de tar med min oldemor Ragnhild, som er snart 99, og farfar Arthur kommer med sin kone, farmor Oddbjørg.
Daisy	Å så bra!
Kristine	Mine tanter og onkler kommer også, med sine barn og barnebarn.
Daisy	Søskenbarna dine?
Kristine	Ja, nettopp. Tante Gunhild, mannen hennes, Aleksander, og deres tre sønner, Elias, Gunnar og Viktor, kommer også snart. Og så kommer onkel Frode med sin kone, Merete, og deres fire barn: tre jenter, Pernille, Iselin og Lisbeth, og én gutt, Kjetil, med datteren på ett år, Helene. Jeg har også to tanter til, tante Sigrid, mammas søster, og hennes samboer, tante Bergljot.
Daisy	Du har en veldig stor familie.
Kristine	Ja, familien vår er ganske stor.
Daisy	Å, jeg gleder meg til å treffe dem!
Kristine	Det blir koselig, hva med din familie? Er den også stor?
Daisy	Nei, ikke så stor, jeg er enebarn og moren min har bare en søster, hun heter Clarissa, og datteren hennes heter Penelope. Faren min har en bror og en søster. Broren hans heter Ciarán, og søsteren hans heter Siobhán. Onkel Ciarán er gift med tante Abigail, og deres datter heter Beatrice. Tante Siobhán og hennes samboer Leroy venter sitt første barn nå, men de vet ikke om det er gutt eller jente.
Kristine	Så spennende! Hva med besteforeldrene dine?
Daisy	Jeg har bare mormoren min igjen, hun heter Faith og er 89 år gammel.

2 Re-read the dialogue above and answer the following questions.

- **a** How many cousins does Kristine have?
- **b** How many cousins does Daisy have?
- **c** How many aunts and uncles does Kristine have?
- **d** How many aunts and uncles does Daisy have?
- **e** How many grandparents and great-grandparents does Kristine have?
- **f** How many grandparents does Daisy have?

3 Look at the conversation again, then match the Norwegian with the English translation.

a Jeg er enebarn og mora mi har bare ei søster.	**1** It will be nice.
b Foreldrene mine kommer, de heter Arne og Inger.	**2** I am an only child and my mother has got only one sister.
c Mine tanter og onkler kommer også.	**3** What about your grandparents?
d Du har en veldig stor familie.	**4** You have a very big family.
e Jeg gleder meg til å treffe dem!	**5** My parents are coming; their names are Arne and Inger.
f Det blir koselig.	**6** I'm looking forward to meeting them!
g Hva med besteforeldrene dine?	**7** My aunts and uncles are also coming.

4 How do Daisy and Kristine say the following?

a only child

1 familie **2** enebarn **3** samboer **4** gift

b partner

1 familie **2** enebarn **3** samboer **4** gift

c married

1 familie **2** enebarn **3** samboer **4** gift

d family

1 familie **2** enebarn **3** samboer **4** gift

5 Underline all the possessive pronouns in the dialogue and answer the following questions.

a How many possessive pronouns can you find?

b What pronouns are used when talking about one's own?

Language discovery 2

POSSESSIVE PRONOUNS

Possessive pronouns in Norwegian can be tricky, so it is very important to have a clear picture of what they mean. Look at the following table and note the differences, then complete the exercise.

Entall – *singular*						Flertall – *plural*	
Hankjønn – *masculine*		Hunkjønn – *feminine*		Intetkjønn – *neuter*		*M–F–N*	
min	*my*	**mi**	*my*	**mitt**	*my*	**mine**	*my*
din	*your(s)*	**di**	*your*	**ditt**	*yours*	**dine**	*yours*
sin	*his / her / its own*	**si**	*his / her / its own*	**sitt**	*his / her / its own*	**sine**	*his / her / its own*
hans	*his*	**hennes**	*her(s)*	**dets**	*its*	**deres**	*their(s)*
vår	*our(s)*	**vår**	*our(s)*	**vårt**	*our(s)*	**våre**	*our(s)*
deres	*your(s)*	**deres**	*your(s)*	**deres**	*your(s)*	**deres**	*your(s)*
sin	*their own*	**si**	*their own*	**sitt**	*their own*	**sine**	*their own*
deres	*their(s)*	**deres**	*their(s)*	**deres**	*their(s)*	**deres**	*their(s)*

1 Translate the following into English.

a Foreldrene mine kommer.
b Min søster heter Astrid.
c Siri er din svigerinne.
d Farfar Arthur kommer med kona si.
e Mine tanter og onkler kommer også med sine barn og barnebarn.
f Tante Gunhild og mannen hennes, Aleksander, kommer med sine tre sønner.
g Og så kommer onkel Frode og kona hans, Merete, og deres fire barn.
h Mammas søster kommer med sin samboer, tante Bergljot.
i Familien vår er ganske stor.
j Mora mi har bare ei søster.
k Tante Siobhán og hennes samboer Leroy venter sitt første barn nå.
l Det er mitt ansvar, ikke ditt!

2 Choose the two correct translations for each of the following expressions.

a my mother
1 mora mi
2 mor mi
3 min mora
4 min mor

b her partner

  1 hennes samboeren

  2 hennes samboer

  3 samboer hennes

  4 samboeren hennes

c your child

  1 ditt barn

  2 barn ditt

  3 ditt barnet

  4 barnet ditt

3 Match the Norwegian with the English translation.

a Han snakker med broren sin.	**1** He's talking to her brother.
b Hun snakker med broren sin.	**2** He's talking to his own brother.
c Han snakker med broren hennes.	**3** She's talking to his brother.
d Hun snakker med broren hennes.	**4** He's talking to his brother.
e Han snakker med broren hans.	**5** She's talking to her own brother.
f Hun snakker med broren hans.	**6** She's talking to her brother.

Practice

1 Read the following text and answer the questions.

Olander og Mia snakker sammen om sine familier. Olander har fire søsken, brødrene hans heter Karl og Johan, og søstrene hans heter Aurora og Margarete. Olander har også mange søskenbarn, og han liker å gå på hyttetur med familien sin. Mia har ei tvillingsøster, hun heter Rachel og bor i London. Mia savner søstera si, men de snakker ofte med hverandre. Familien til Mia kommer snart til Norge på besøk, og Mia gleder seg veldig mye til det.

a What are Mia and Olander talking about?

b How many siblings does Olander have?

c Does Mia have a brother?

d Does Mia miss her family?

e What is Mia's family soon going to do?

f Is Mia happy about it?

2 **Write a short text in which you talk about your family.**

3 **Write a short summary of the second dialogue.**

Test yourself

1 Translate the following sentences.

a I have one stepsister and two brothers.
b She is my aunt.
c My uncle has two children.
d Her grandfather is 98 years old.
e His wife's name is Astrid.
f My female cousin is 20 years old.

2 Rearrange the words into sentences; don't forget to place the capital letter on the first word.

a	gammel	hun	hvor	er	?			
b	fetter	er	mellom	forskjellen	hva	kusine	og	?
c	mor	min	Laura	heter	.			
d	Tromsø	kommer	Gudrun	broren	fra	og	Ola	til
	er	.						

3 Answer the following questions with information about yourself and your family.

a Har du noen søsken?
b Hvor mange søskenbarn har du?
c Hvor mange barn har du?
d Hva heter foreldrene dine?
e Hvor mange onkler og tanter har du?

SELF CHECK

	I CAN ...
○	... talk about my family.
○	... use different possessive forms.
○	... talk about days, months and seasons.
○	... ask what things are called in Norwegian.

5

In this unit, you will learn how to:

» find out how much things cost and talk about the quantity and quality of objects.
» talk about size and colors when buying clothes.
» use modal verbs and the future tense.
» state opinions and talk about likes and dislikes.

Vi skal handle!

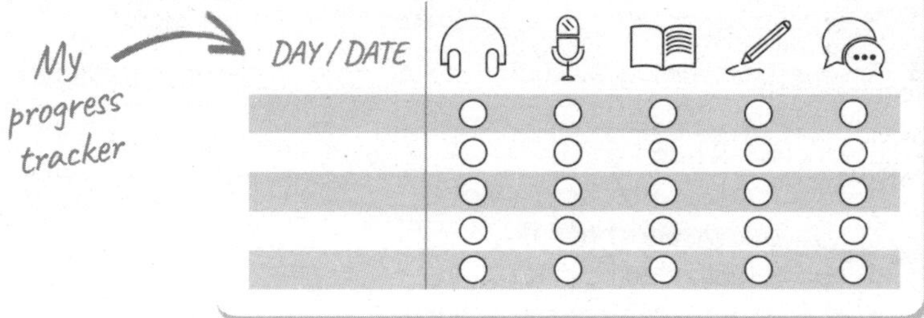

Buying and selling

The Norwegian currency is called **kroner**, or **NOK** (*Norwegian Crown*). There are **mynter** (*coins*) and **sedler** (*notes*); however, in Norway it is very common **å betale med kort** (*to pay by card*) even for cheaper items. When you **kjøper** (*buy*) something, you receive a **kvittering** (*receipt*) and if you buy groceries, you are usually asked if you need to buy a **pose** (*bag*). In Norway **priser** (*prices*) are quite **høye** (*high*), and things are **dyre** (*expensive*). If you need **å spare penger** (*to save money*), and are looking for something **billig** (*cheap*), you can **se etter** (*look for*) **tilbud** (*discounts*) and **salg** (*sales*).

---

a What do the words høye and dyre have in common?

b Can you tell if they are plural or singular? How?

Vocabulary builder

05.01 Listen to the following words and then repeat, trying to imitate the Norwegian pronunciation. Then complete the missing English translations.

CLOTHES

bluse (ei)	_______
bobledress (en)	*quilted overall (commonly worn in Norway)*
bukse (en) / bukser	*trouser(s)*
genser (en)	*sweater / jumper*
hanske (en)	*glove(s)*
hatt (en)	_______
jakke (ei)	_______
kjole (en)	*dress*
lue (ei)	*beret*
regnjakke (ei)	*rain jacket*
skjerf (et)	*scarf*
skjorte (ei)	*shirt*
skjørt (et)	*skirt*
sko (en)	*shoe(s)*
sokk (en)	_______
strømpebukse (en)	*tights*
støvel (en)	*boot(s)*
t-skjorte (ei)	_______
ullgenser (en)	*woollen sweater*
vott (en)	*mitten(s)*

LANGUAGE TIP

Beware of false friends! In Norwegian, **en dress** means *a suit*, and **et slips** means *a tie*.

COLORS

blå	_______
grønn	_______
grå	_______
gul	*yellow*
hvit	*white*
lilla	*lilac*

fiolett	*violet*
oransje	*orange*
rosa	*pink*
rød	________
svart	*black*

NEW EXPRESSIONS

Some of these new expressions are used in the following dialogues. Note their meanings and the differences between the various alternatives.

AT THE SHOP

Hva koster det?	*How much does it cost? (lit. What does it cost?)*
Hvor mye blir det?	*How much is it?*
Hvor mye koster det?	*How much does it cost?*
Vil du ha en pose?	*Do you want a bag?*
Vil du ha kvitteringen?	*Do you want the receipt?*
Hvor er prøverommet?	*Where is the fitting room?*
Hvilken størrelse er det?	*What size is this?*
Finnes det/den i flere farger?	*Does it come in more colors?*
Det stemmer.	*That's right.*

Dialogue 1

05.02 *Sara needs to buy a present for her friend's birthday so she goes to the store with Nora to find something. Listen carefully to the dialogue before answering the questions.*

1 What do Sara and Nora buy Hanna for her birthday?

2 How much is it?

Sara	Vi må kjøpe noe til Hanna. Skal vi kjøpe henne en fin genser?
Nora	Jeg vet ikke helt, hun liker bare sportsklær. Det er alltid så vanskelig å finne gaver til henne.
Sara	Ja, du har rett, vi kan kjøpe et par hansker, hva synes du?
Nora	Nei, hun har hansker og de er helt nye. Hva med en lue?
Sara	Ja, det er en god idé. Hvilken lue? Denne eller denne?
Nora	Hun liker ikke rosa. Finnes det ikke i flere farger?
Sara	Jo, de finnes i blå og grønn, eller i grå. Hvor mye koster de?
Nora	De koster 299 kroner per stykke.
Sara	Det er ikke så billig, men det går fint. Vi tar den i blå og grønn, den andre er kjedelig.
Nora	Jeg er enig. Kan vi få se på genserne? Jeg vil gjerne kjøpe noe nytt for meg selv.
Sara	Ja, vi kan sikkert gjøre det.
Nora	Jeg bør prøve denne genseren. Hvor er prøverommene?
Sara	De er der borte.

3 Listen again to the dialogue and answer the following questions.

- **a** Where are Nora and Sara doing shopping?
- **b** Why do they not buy gloves for Hanna?
- **c** Where are the fitting rooms?

4 Match the Norwegian with the English translation.

- **a** Jeg bør prøve denne genseren.
- **b** Vi må kjøpe noe til Hanna.
- **c** Skal vi kjøpe henne en fin genser?
- **d** Kan vi se på genserne?
- **e** Jeg vil gjerne kjøpe noe nytt for meg selv.

1. Can we look at the sweaters?
2. I should try this sweater on.
3. Should we buy her a nice sweater?
4. I would like to buy something new for myself.
5. We have to buy something for Hanna.

5 What words do Nora and Sara use for the following?

a presents

1 sikkert **2** gaver **3** farger

b colors

1 sikkert **2** gaver **3** farger

c surely

1 sikkert **2** gaver **3** farger

6 Choose the correct translation for the following expressions with *to like* **and** *would like***.**

a She only likes sporty clothes.

1 Jeg vil gjerne kjøpe noe nytt.
2 Hun liker bare sportsklær.
3 Hun liker ikke rosa.

b She does not like pink.

1 Jeg vil gjerne kjøpe noe nytt.
2 Hun liker bare sportsklær.
3 Hun liker ikke rosa.

c I would really like to buy something new.

1 Jeg vil gjerne kjøpe noe nytt.
2 Hun liker bare sportsklær.
3 Hun liker ikke rosa.

Language discovery 1

1 MODAL VERBS

Modal verbs are verbs which usually accompany other verbs and give additional information about them. They also express possibility, obligation, necessity and intention.

1 Read Dialogue 1 again and find the expressions that mean:

a We have to (must) buy something.
b I want to buy something for myself.
c I should try it on.
d Shall we buy her a sweater?

Norwegian modal verbs are similar to English modal verbs, with the exception of the verb **å skulle** (and sometimes **å ville**), which is also used to express a future intention:

INFINITIVE	PRESENT TENSE	ENGLISH
å skulle	**jeg / du / etc. ... skal**	*shall / will*
å måtte	**jeg / du / etc. ... må**	*must / have to*
å ville	**jeg / du / etc. ... vil**	*want / will*
å burde	**jeg / du / etc. ... bør**	*should*
å kunne	**jeg / du / etc. ... kan**	*can*

Modal verbs behave differently from other verbs: they do not take the **-r** ending in the present tense, but they are still the same whatever the subject is (see Unit 1). In Norwegian, modal verbs are always followed by another verb in the infinite form without the **å**.

Hun *vil ha* en kopp kaffe. *She would like (lit. she wants) to have a cup of coffee.*

Du *må gå* nå. *You have to leave now.*

Han *bør lese*. *He should study.*

***Skal* jeg *åpne* vinduet?** *Shall I open the window?*

***Kan* du *ringe* meg i morgen?** *Can you call me tomorrow?*

2 THE FUTURE TENSE

In Norwegian, there are several ways to talk about the future:

Skal + verb

Vi *skal* (reise)* til Roma i morgen. *We will leave for Rome tomorrow.*

*Motion verbs can be omitted in the future tense with **skal**. This is the only time when it is possible to omit the verb. No other verbs can be omitted.

Jeg *skal* ringe deg snart. *I will call you soon.*

Present tense

Vi *reiser* i morgen. *We are leaving tomorrow.*

Flyet *kommer* kl. 16.40. *The plane lands at 16.40.*

Det *blir* fint å se dere igjen. *It will be nice to see you again.*

Kommer til å + verb

Det *kommer til å* regne snart.	*It is going to rain soon.*
Det *kommer til å* bli en koselig kveld.	*It is going to be a cosy/nice evening/night.*

Vil + verb

Det *vil* vise seg at jeg har rett.	*You'll see that I'm right.*
Det *vil* skje snart.	*It's going to happen soon.*

2 Match the Norwegian with the English translation.

a Vi skal reise i morgen.	**1** It's going to rain soon.
b Det kommer til å regne snart.	**2** The train leaves at noon.
c Han drar i morgen.	**3** I will call you tomorrow.
d Flyet kommer kl. 16.40.	**4** He's leaving tomorrow.
e Det vil skje snart.	**5** We will leave tomorrow.
f Toget drar kl. 12.00.	**6** The plane lands at 16.40.
g Jeg ringer deg i morgen.	**7** It's going to happen soon.

Dialogue 2

05.03 *Bente and Tore meet Michelle, their French neighbor, at the hall of residence, and they talk about what they are going to do tomorrow. Listen carefully to the dialogue before answering the questions.*

1 What are Tore and Bente going to do tomorrow?

2 Does Michelle know the band?

Bente og Tore	Hei Michelle, hvordan går det?
Michelle	Det går veldig bra, takk. Hva med dere?
Bente	Det går bra med oss også, takk.
Tore	Ja, det gjør det, vi skal på konsert i morgen.
Michelle	Å, så bra! Hvilket band er det som spiller?
Bente	Det er vårt favorittband ...
Tore	Kaizers Orchestra.
Michelle	Å, jeg synes de er fantastiske! Hvor spiller de?
Bente	De skal spille på Operaen.
Tore	Det kommer til å bli supert!
Michelle	Ja, det blir det sikkert.
Tore	Vil du bli med?
Bente	Ja! Det er en flott idé, kom!
Michelle	Gjerne det, takk.
Bente	Bra! Da skal vi kjøpe én billett til.
Michelle	Å nei, vent! Jeg jobber i morgen.
Tore	Nei, det er synd.
Michelle	Ja, men kanskje neste gang ...

3 Re-read the dialogue and answer the following questions.

a What do they ask Michelle?

b What does she answer at first?

c Then what does she say?

4 Look at the conversation again, then match the Norwegian with the English translation.

a	Vil du bli med?	**1**	It's a pity.
b	Det er en flott idé!	**2**	Do you want to come with us?
c	Da skal vi kjøpe én billett til.	**3**	It's a wonderful idea!
d	Det er synd.	**4**	Then we'll buy one more ticket.

5 How do Bente, Tore and Michelle say the following?

a group

1 supert **2** billett **3** band **4** kanskje

b wonderful

1 supert **2** kanskje **3** gjerne **4** flott

c great

1 supert **2** kanskje **3** gjerne **4** flott

d gladly

1 supert **2** kanskje **3** gjerne **4** flott

e ticket

1 billett **2** band **3** kanskje **4** gjerne

f maybe

1 supert **2** kanskje **3** gjerne **4** flott

Language discovery 2

1 ADJECTIVES (INDEFINITE)

Norwegian adjectives are placed before the noun. If the noun is plural, then the adjective becomes plural. For example, in English we say *red hats*, but in Norwegian it becomes *reds hats* (**røde hatter**). The adjective will also change depending on whether the noun is masculine, feminine or neuter; for example, **en blå genser**, **ei blå lue**, **et blått skjerf**.

Masculine and feminine

When adjectives do not take any ending, they are in the basic form. The basic form is used when the adjective describes words that have **en** (masculine) and **ei** (feminine) in front.

1 Match the Norwegian with the English translation.

a	en fin genser	**1**	a cheap beret
b	en rød genser	**2**	a cheap hat
c	en norsk gutt	**3**	a green beret
d	en billig hatt	**4**	a green sweater
e	en grønn genser	**5**	a new (female) friend
f	en ny venn	**6**	a new friend
g	ei fin jente	**7**	a nice girl
h	ei rød lampe	**8**	a nice sweater
i	ei norsk jente	**9**	a Norwegian boy
j	ei billig lue	**10**	a Norwegian girl
k	ei ny venninne	**11**	a red lamp
l	ei grønn lue	**12**	a red sweater

Neuter

When the adjective describes a word that has **et** in front (neuter), the adjective has a **-t** added at the end:

2 Complete the adjective with the right ending.

a et fin________ hus — *a nice house*
b et rød________ hus — *a red house*
c et grøn________ eple — *a green apple*

When the basic form is short and contains only one vowel, the adjective has **-tt** added at the end of the neuter form:

3 Complete the adjective with the right ending.

a et ny________ hus — *a new house*
b et blå________ skjerf — *a blue scarf*

However, some adjectives may use the basic form also for neuter words:

- if an adjective ends in **-sk**.
- if an adjective ends in **-ig**.
- if an adjective ends in **-e**.

Look at the following examples:

et *norsk* hus — *a Norwegian house*
et *fantastisk* liv — *a fantastic life*
et *moderne* hus — *a modern house*
et *billig* skjerf — *a cheap scarf*

Plural

When the adjective describes a plural word, the adjective has an **-e** added at the end:

4 Match the Norwegian with the English translation.

a røde gensere	**1** cheap clothes
b fine gensere	**2** green shoes
c røde lamper	**3** new friends
d fine lamper	**4** nice houses
e røde hus	**5** nice lamps
f fine hus	**6** nice sweaters
g norske flagg	**7** Norwegian flags
h billige klær	**8** red houses
i nye venner	**9** red lamps
j grønne sko	**10** red sweaters

When using the verb

When we describe things by using adjectives, we can also say that something is *good / bad / beautiful*, etc. by putting the adjective after the verb. When doing this, the noun has to be in the definite form (so not **en gutt** but **gutten**, etc.).

5 Choose the right translation for the following sentences.

a The boy is tired.
  1 Gutt er trøtt. **2** Gutten er trøtt.

b The jacket is nice.
  1 Jakka er fin. **2** Jakke er fin.

c The bread is fresh.
  1 Brød er ferskt. **2** Brødet er ferskt.

d The buns are good.
  1 Bollene er gode. **2** Bolle er gode.

EXCEPTIONS

Some adjectives behave in a different way and change completely depending on whether the noun they describe is masculine, feminine, neuter or plural. Look at the examples below and note the differences.

en annen gutt	*another boy*	**en liten gutt**	*a little boy*
ei anna jente	*another girl*	**ei lita jente**	*a little girl*
et annet hus	*another house*	**et lite hus**	*a small house*
andre folk	*other people*	**små barn**	*small children*

2 ADJECTIVES (DEFINITE)

If the adjective comes after a possessive pronoun (**min**, **mitt**, **din**, **ditt**, etc.), or after a demonstrative pronoun (**den**, **det**, **denne**, **dette**, etc.), it has an **-e** added at the end, as with the plural form.

In Norwegian, there is a rule called double determination (**dobbelt bestemmelse**), which means that when there is an adjective between the definite article and the noun, both the adjective and the noun have to be in the definite form:

den* slitne gutt*en	*the tired boy*
den* vakre kvinn*en	*the beautiful woman*
det* pene barn*et	*the beautiful child*
de* dyre sko*ene	*the expensive shoes*

This does not work for possessive forms. Then, the noun remains in the indefinite form:

***mitt* store hus**	*my big house*
***hans* nye hund**	*his new dog*
Lars' nye bil	*Lars' new car*

6 Look at the examples and choose the correct Norwegian translation.

a my new house
 1 mitt store hus
 2 mitt stort hus

b the beautiful woman
 1 den vakker kvinnen
 2 den vakre kvinnen

c The bread is fresh.
 1 Brødet er ferskt.
 2 Brødet er fersk.

d The boy is kind.
 1 Gutt er snill.
 2 Gutten er snill.

e a nice house
 1 et fint hus
 2 et fine hus

f a red lamp
 1 ei røde lampe
 2 ei rød lampe

g a Norwegian girl
 1 ei norsk jente
 2 ei norske jente

h a cheap scarf
 1 et billigt skjerf
 2 et billig skjerf

i expensive clothes
 1 dyrt klær
 2 dyre klær

Practice

1 05.04 **Listen to Maja describing what she is wearing today and what she likes wearing, then read the text out loud and answer the questions.**

I dag har jeg på meg en lyseblå t-skjorte, en mørkegrå genser, et grønt skjørt, en svart strømpebukse og mørkegrå sko. Så har jeg på meg en rød jakke, svarte votter og et lilla skjerf. Jeg er veldig glad i å bruke skjørt og jeg gjør det ofte, selv om det er kaldt ute. Jeg liker både lyse og mørke farger, men jeg synes mørke farger kan være kjedelige noen ganger. Jeg hater å bruke høyhælte sko.

- **a** How does she say *I am wearing ...*?
- **b** How does she say *I love wearing a skirt*?
- **c** How does she say *I like ...*?
- **d** How does she say *I hate ...*?
- **e** What words does Maja use to talk about light and dark?

LANGUAGE TIP

In Norwegian there are various ways to say that we *love, hate, like something or someone*. Look at the list and note the differences in use:

å elske *to love*
å hate *to hate*
å like *to like*
å mislike *to dislike*
å være glad i noen *to care for someone (lit. to be happy in someone)*

2 Re-read the text and answer the following questions.

- **a** What is Maja wearing?
- **b** What colors is she wearing?
- **c** What is Maja's opinion about colors?
- **d** What does she hate wearing?
- **e** What does she think of skirts?

3 Read the following story and fill in the blanks with the right adjectives, choosing from the list below. (More than one answer can be correct.)

fantastisk – flink – gammel – hvit – hyggelige – koselig – liten – morsom – pen – smart – snill – solrik – stor – stort – ung

a Kristin er en ________ kvinne.

b Hun er 24 år ________ , hun er ________ og hun studerer fysikk, fordi hun er ________ .

c Hun har en ________ hund og en ________ katt, og de bor på Frogner i Oslo.

d Huset der de bor er ________ , men det er ikke så ________ .

e Hagen er ________ og ________ , og hun sitter ofte der og leser fordi det er ________ .

f Kristin har mange ________ venner, og hun er veldig ________ og ________ , og har alltid noen på besøk.

g Hun synes livet er ________ !

4 Now write another story using new adjectives.

____

____

____

____

____

Test yourself

1 Translate the following into Norwegian.

a an expensive jacket
b a blue scarf
c the clever girl
d green gloves
e a cheap sweater
f the kind boy

2 Fill in the blanks with the correct modal verb.

a Du ________ lese i dag.
b Jeg ________ kjøpe nye sko.
c Haris ________ til Berlin neste mandag.
d ________ du hjelpe meg?
e Hun ________ ikke jobbe her.

3 Describe what you are wearing today.

____

____

____

4 Complete the following sentences by putting the words in the correct order. The first word is already in the correct position.

a	*I dag*	meg	på	en	har	lyseblå	jeg	t-skjorte	.
b	*Så*	på	har	rød	jeg	jakke	meg	ei	.
c	*Nå*	Oslo	i	jeg	bor	.			
d	*Nå*	Stavanger	ikke	bor	i	Hans	.		

SELF CHECK

	I CAN ...
○	... go shopping and talk about prices.
○	... use adjectives to describe what I'm wearing.

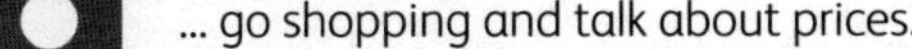

6

In this unit, you will learn how to:

» talk about the time and describe your daily routine.
» use time expressions.
» use prepositional verbs, reflexive verbs and reflexive pronouns.
» use verbs of movement and adverbs of place.

Hva gjør du hver dag?

My progress tracker

DAY / DATE	Listen	Speak	Read	Write	Converse
	○	○	○	○	○
	○	○	○	○	○
	○	○	○	○	○
	○	○	○	○	○
	○	○	○	○	○

Time of the day

In Norwegian, to talk about **tid** (*time*) we use the expression **klokka / klokken er** (*the clock is*), then the minutes, then **over** (*past*) from 1 to 19 minutes past the hour. For example, 12.10 will be **klokka er ti over tolv** – *ten past twelve*, 12.05 will be **klokka er fem over tolv**, etc. From 41 minutes past to 1 minute to the following hour we use **på** (*to*). For example, 12.50 will be **klokka er ti på ett** – *ten to one*, 12.55 will be **klokka er fem på ett**, etc. To talk about 12.15 and 12.45 we say, respectively, **klokka er kvart over tolv** (*a quarter past twelve*) and **klokka er kvart på ett** (*a quarter to one*). To say 12.30 in Norwegian we say **halv ett** (literally *half one*, meaning that there are 30 minutes left before the following hour). From 20 to 29 past we use **på halv** (*to half*) + the following hour, and from 31 to 40 we use **over halv** (*past half*) + the following hour. This is especially difficult when making appointments, because one risks arriving one hour late. If you are not saying what time it is, but that you have to meet someone **klokka** (*clock*) **ti over halv ett**, it means you are meeting them at 12.40 (literally *ten minutes after half past twelve*). While if you have to meet them at **klokka ti på halv ett**, you are meeting them at 12.20 (literally *ten minutes before half past twelve*). To ask what time it is, we have several options: **Hva er klokka?** (lit. *what is the clock (time)?*); **Hvor mye er klokka (blitt)?** (lit. *how much is the clock / has the clock become?*); **Hvor mange er klokka?** (lit. *how many hours is the clock?*).

What do the following sentences mean?

a Klokka er ti over fire. **b Vi treffes klokka halv tre.**

LANGUAGE TIP

Note that the time can be written with or without the full stop: 16.30 or 1630

Vocabulary builder

06.01 Listen to the following verbs, and then repeat, trying to imitate the Norwegian pronunciation. Then complete with the missing meanings in English.

å bli	*to become / to stay*
å dra	*to go (using a means of transport but not driving it)*
å drikke	______
å dusje	*to shower*
å fly	______
å gjøre	*to do*
å gå	*to walk*
å kjøre	*to drive*
å komme	______
å lage	*to make*
å ligge	______
å reise	*to travel*
å sitte	______
å spise	*to eat*
å stå	*to stand*
å ta	______

NEW EXPRESSIONS

Some of these new expressions are used in the following dialogues. Note their meaning and the differences between the various alternatives.

Jeg står opp.	*I get up.*
Jeg våkner (opp).	*I wake up.*

Jeg vekker deg.	*I wake you up.*
Jeg kler på meg.	*I get dressed.*
Jeg tar på meg jakke.	*I wear a jacket.*
Jeg har på meg lue.	*I am wearing a hat.*
Jeg legger meg tidlig.	*I go to bed early.*
Jeg kommer for sent.	*I arrive late.*
Jeg liker å sove lenge.	*I like sleeping late.*
Jeg bor langt fra jobben min.	*I live far from my workplace.*
Hvor lang tid tar det?	*How long does it take?*

Dialogue 1

06.02 *Sigrid and Karl describe their daily routine to each other. Listen carefully to the dialogue before answering the questions.*

1 At what time do Sigrid and Karl get up in the morning?

2 How do they go to work?

Karl	Hva gjør du om morgenen?
Sigrid	Jeg står opp kl. 06.45, så tar jeg en dusj og kler på meg. Etterpå spiser jeg frokost og drar på jobb. Hva med deg?
Karl	Jeg liker å sove lenge om morgenen, men jeg må være på jobb kl. 9, så jeg står opp kl. 07.30. Først spiser jeg frokost og så dusjer jeg og kler på meg. Etterpå går jeg på jobb. Jeg bor nær jobben min, så jeg trenger ikke å kjøre.
Sigrid	Å, det er deilig! Jeg bor ganske langt fra jobben min, først må jeg gå, så må jeg ta T-banen og etterpå må jeg ta bussen.
Karl	Oi, hvor lang tid tar det?
Sigrid	Nesten en time.
Karl	Hvorfor kjører du ikke bil?
Sigrid	Fordi jeg må kjøpe en ny bil først. Men når det blir fint vær vil jeg prøve å sykle.
Karl	Ja, det er en god idé! Hva gjør du etter jobben?
Sigrid	Jeg blir ferdig på jobb kl. 16.30, så drar jeg hjem, skifter klær og handler mat. Jeg går på tyskkurs én gang i uken, og noen ganger treffer jeg venner etter kurset, eller etter jobben, så kommer jeg hjem og legger meg tidlig. Hva med deg?

Karl	Jeg er ferdig kl. 17.00, og så tar jeg en tur i skogen for å nyte naturen. Etterpå kommer jeg hjem og lager mat, og noen ganger inviterer jeg venner til middag hos meg. Etter middagen ser jeg på TV eller hører på musikk mens jeg leser en bok. Jeg liker ikke å legge meg veldig tidlig.
Sigrid	Jeg skjønner, jeg liker det ikke heller, men jeg må det uansett.

3 Listen again to the dialogue and answer the following questions.

- **a** When does Karl have to be at work?
- **b** What does Karl like doing in the morning?
- **c** Why does Sigrid not drive to work?
- **d** What does Sigrid do after work?
- **e** What does Karl do after work?

4 Look at the conversation again, then match the Norwegian with the English translation.

- **a** Fordi jeg må kjøpe en ny bil først.
- **b** Etterpå går jeg på jobb.
- **c** Jeg liker det ikke heller.
- **d** Jeg blir ferdig på jobb klokka 16.30.
- **e** Når det blir fint vær vil jeg prøve å sykle.

1. I finish work at 16.30.
2. Because I have to buy a new car first.
3. When the weather gets better I want to try to cycle.
4. I don't like it either.
5. Afterwards I go to work.

CULTURE TIP

After **pandemien** (*the COVID pandemic*) many Norwegian **arbeidsgivere** (*employers*) have maintained **hjemmekontor** (*working from home, lit. home office*) for at least a few days a week.

5 What words do Sigrid and Karl use for the following?

a neither
1. én gang i uka
2. ganske
3. heller
4. langt

b almost
1. nesten
2. noen ganger
3. nær
4. uansett

c near
1. nesten
2. noen ganger
3. nær
4. uansett

d rather
1. én gang i uka
2. ganske
3. heller
4. langt

e anyway
1 nesten
2 noen ganger
3 nær
4 uansett

f far
1 én gang i uka
2 ganske
3 heller
4 langt

g once a week
1 én gang i uka
2 ganske
3 heller
4 langt

h sometimes
1 nesten
2 noen ganger
3 nær
4 uansett

6 Choose the correct translation for each of these expressions.

a I get dressed.
1 Jeg våkner.
2 Jeg kler på meg.
3 Jeg står opp.
4 Jeg legger meg.

b I go to bed.
1 Jeg våkner.
2 Jeg kler på meg.
3 Jeg står opp.
4 Jeg legger meg.

c I get up.
1 Jeg våkner.
2 Jeg kler på meg.
3 Jeg står opp.
4 Jeg legger meg.

d I wake up.
1 Jeg våkner.
2 Jeg kler på meg.
3 Jeg står opp.
4 Jeg legger meg.

Language discovery 1

1 TIME EXPRESSIONS

In Norwegian, we can use time expressions both at the beginning and at the end of a sentence. If used at the beginning of a sentence, then the sentence structure should follow that of a question, with the verb and subject changing places.

Nå <u>bor jeg</u> i Bergen.	*Now I live in Bergen*
<u>Jeg bor</u> i Bergen **nå**.	*I live in Bergen now.*

Adverbs of time

først	*first(ly)*
så	*then*
etterpå	*afterwards*
før	*before*
etter	*after*

LANGUAGE TIP

We also have to bear in mind that **før** and **etter** always have to be accompanied by something (i.e. what happened before or after), while **først** and **etterpå** can be used alone. Look at the following examples:

***Før* frokost dusjer jeg.**	*Before breakfast, I take a shower.*
***Etter* jobb tar jeg en tur i skogen.**	*After work, I take a walk in the woods.*
***Først* dusjer jeg, *så* spiser jeg frokost.**	*I take a shower first, and then I eat breakfast.*
Vi sees *etterpå*.	*See you later.*

1 Look at the following list of things that Sverre has to do during the day. Fill in the blanks below with the correct adverbs of time.

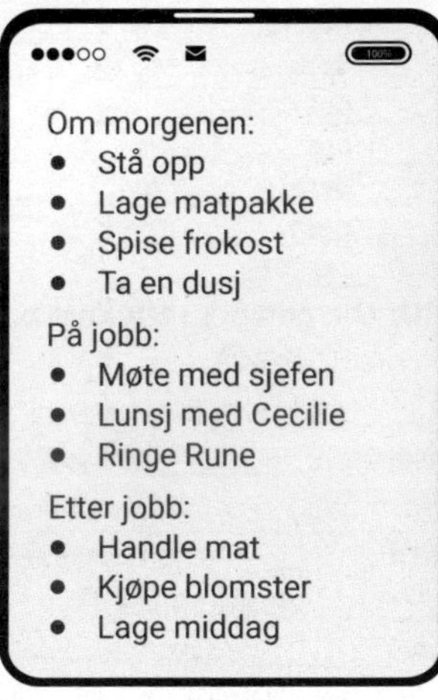

a ________ står han opp, ________ lager han matpakke.

b ________ spiser han frokost, ________ tar han en dusj.

c Han spiser lunsj med Cecilie ________ møtet med sjefen.

d ________ ringer han Rune.

e ________ jobb handler han mat, ________ kjøper han blomster. ________ lager han middag.

2 REFLEXIVE PRONOUNS AND VERBS

As you may have noticed in the last dialogue, some verbs are accompanied by a reflexive pronoun, which refers back to the subject. Look at the following examples and then study the table.

Jeg legger meg tidlig. *I go to bed early. (lit. I lie myself down early.)*

Han soler seg. *He is getting a tan.*

Skynd deg. *Hurry up! (lit. Hurry yourself.)*

Subject		Object		Reflexive	
jeg	*I*	**meg**	*me*	**meg**	*myself*
du	*you*	**deg**	*you*	**deg**	*yourself*
han	*he*	**ham / han**	*him*	**seg**	*himself*
hun	*she*	**henne**	*her*		*herself*
den *(non-neuter)* **det** *(neuter)*	*it*	**den** **det**	*it*		*itself*
vi	*we*	**oss**	*us*	**oss**	*ourselves*
dere	*you*	**dere**	*you*	**dere**	*yourselves*
de	*they*	**dem**	*them*	**seg**	*themselves*

2 Fill in the blanks with the correct reflexive pronoun.

- **a** Hun liker _______ der. (*herself*)
- **b** Jenta ønsker _______ en hund. (*herself*)
- **c** Jeg trenger å konsentrere _______ . (*myself*)
- **d** Kos _______ . (*yourselves*)
- **e** De har ikke bestemt _______ . (*themselves*)
- **f** Du må oppføre _______ pent. (*yourself*)
- **g** Har dere skjerf med _______ ? (*yourselves*)
- **h** Jeg legger _______ tidlig. (*myself*)
- **i** Han soler _______ . (*himself*)
- **j** Skynd _______ . (*yourself*)

Dialogue 2

06.03 *Astrid and Odin are making plans to meet Ida after school. Listen carefully to their dialogue and answer the following questions.*

1 When are they meeting?

2 Why can't they meet right after Ida has finished her lesson?

Astrid	Hvor skal vi treffe Ida da?
Odin	Jeg vet ikke, vi kan treffes foran biblioteket, hva synes du?
Astrid	Ja, men jeg vet ikke hvor hun kommer fra.
Odin	Hun er ferdig med forelesning kl. 10.30, og hun kommer fra kjemibygningen.
Astrid	Når er du ferdig?
Odin	I morgen er jeg hjemme, for jeg har ikke forelesning, så jeg kommer med trikken. Å treffes foran biblioteket passer fint for meg. Og etterpå kan vi ta T-banen ned til sentrum.
Astrid	Ok. Men jeg er ikke ferdig før kl. 12, kan vi treffes 12.15?
Odin	Ja, ikke noe problem for meg. Jeg sier ifra til Ida så sees vi kl. 12.15 foran biblioteket. Vi kan sitte der og lese mens vi venter på deg.
Astrid	Tusen takk.
Odin	Bare hyggelig, vi ses i morgen.
Astrid	Ja, ha det!

3 Re-read the dialogue above and answer the questions.

a Where are they going to meet?

b How will Odin come to the meeting?

c When do Astrid's lectures end?

d When are they going to meet?

4 Look at the conversation again, then match the Norwegian with the English translation.

a Vi kan sitte der og lese mens vi venter på deg.
b Jeg er ikke ferdig før klokka 12.
c Hun er ferdig med forelesning klokka 10.30.
d I morgen er jeg hjemme, for jeg har ikke forelesning.
e Bare hyggelig, vi ses i morgen.
f Når er du ferdig?
g Jeg vet ikke hvor hun kommer fra.
h Etterpå kan vi ta T-banen ned til sentrum.

1 When will you be finished?
2 Afterwards we can take the subway down to the center.
3 No problem, see you tomorrow.
4 I don't know where she comes from.
5 We can sit there and study while we wait for you.
6 Her lessons end at 10.30.
7 I'm not finished until 12.
8 I'm home tomorrow, because I don't have any lessons.

5 How do Astrid and Odin say the following?

a in front of
1 etterpå **2** ferdig **3** foran **4** hjemme

b when
1 foran **2** hjemme **3** mens **4** når

c finished
1 ferdig **2** foran **3** hjemme **4** når

d at home
1 etterpå **2** ferdig **3** hjemme **4** mens

e afterwards
1 etterpå **2** hjemme **3** mens **4** når

f while
1 etterpå **2** ferdig **3** mens **4** når

Language discovery 2

1 VERBS OF MOVEMENT

In Norwegian there is no equivalent of the *-ing* form, so to say that something is happening we can use the present tense (see Unit 1). Another typical thing to do is use another verb to describe our physical position while doing something else. Look at the examples:

Hanne *sitter og ser* på TV.	*Hanne is sitting and watching TV.*
Magnus *står og venter* på bussen.	*Magnus is standing and waiting for the bus.*
Barnet *ligger og sover*.	*The child is lying (down) and sleeping.*
Vi *sitter og snakker*.	*We are sitting and chatting.*

1 Fill in the blanks with the correct verb.

a Hanne ________ og ________ på TV. (*sit, watch*)
b Du ________ og ________ ei bok. (*lie (down), read*)
c Jeg ________ og ________ på telefon. (*stand, talk*)
d Magnus ________ og ________ på bussen. (*sit, wait*)
e Guro ________ og ________ på vinduene. (*walk, look at*)
f Barnet ________ og ________ . (*lie (down), sleep*)
g Vi ________ og ________ . (*stand, talk*)

2 ADVERBS OF PLACE

As we saw in Unit 4, Norwegian adverbs of place change depending on whether the verb they follow indicates a static condition or dynamic action. Look at the following table and note the differences:

Motion		State	
Vi går *hjem*.	*We go home.*	**Vi er *hjemme*.**	*We are home.*
Han går *ned*.	*He goes down(stairs).*	**Han er *nede*.**	*He is down(stairs).*
Hun går *opp*.	*She goes up(stairs).*	**Hun er *oppe*.**	*She is up(stairs).*
Du går *inn*.	*You go in.*	**Du er *inne*.**	*You are inside.*
Jeg går *ut*.	*I go out.*	**Jeg er *ute*.**	*I am outside.*

2 Fill in the blanks with the correct adverb of place.

HJEMME / HJEM

a Hanna er ________ hele dagen i dag.
b Gro drar ________ snart.

INNE / INN

c Hvor er Magnus? Han sitter ________.
d Gå ________ og ta et glass vann.

UTE / UT

e Barna leker ________ hele dagen om sommeren.
f Gå ________ nå!

NEDE / NED

g Jeg går ________.

h Hun sitter ________.

OPPE / OPP

i Hvor er katten? Han sover ________.

j Gå ________ og ta en dusj.

Practice

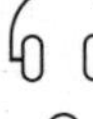

1 06.04 **Listen to Johan describing his weekly routine, then read the text out loud.**

Jeg jobber hver dag fra mandag til fredag. Jeg står alltid opp kl. 07.30, jeg spiser frokost først, så tar jeg en dusj, kler på meg og drar på jobb. Jeg er ferdig på jobb mellom kl. 16.30 og 17.00. Etterpå drar jeg hjem, eller treffer noen venner i byen. Noen ganger går vi på kino, eller spiser middag sammen, men jeg legger meg alltid tidlig når jeg jobber. Jeg jobber aldri på lørdag og jeg reiser ofte bort i helgene.

a How does Johan say *every day*?

b How does he say *never*?

c How does he say *often*?

d How does he say *always*?

e How does he say *sometimes*?

2 Re-read the text and answer the following questions.

a What does Johan do during the week?

1 He goes to work every day.

2 He goes to the cinema every afternoon.

3 He goes to bed late every night.

b When does he get up?

1 At half past eight.

2 At half past six.

3 At half past seven.

c What does he do after work?

1 He goes home or meets some friends in the city.

2 He goes home and goes to bed.

3 He goes home to some friends.

d What does he usually do during the weekend?

1 He goes to concerts.

2 He meets friends.

3 He travels.

3 Write a short text in which you describe an afternoon in the city with a tourist friend of yours.

4 Rearrange the words into sentences; don't forget to place the capital letter on the first word.

a	legger	jeg	tidlig	meg	.		
b	barnet	hund	seg	ønsker	en	.	
c	ikke	de	bestemt	seg	har	.	
d	står	bussen	venter	Magnus	og	på	.
e	sover	barnet	og	ligger	.		

5 Write a short summary of the first dialogue.

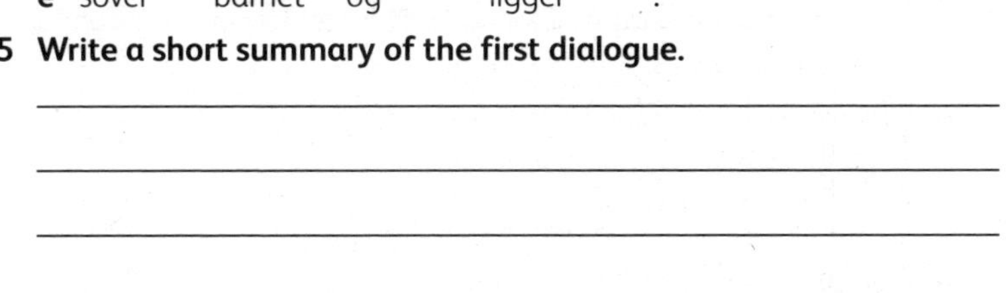

Test yourself

1 Translate the following sentences into Norwegian and say them out loud.

a I eat breakfast before going to work.
b I go to work by bus.
c After work, I go to a German course.
d See you later.
e First, I buy groceries, and then I go home and read a book.
f I'm standing here waiting for you.

2 Fill in the blanks with the correct verb. There is more than one possible answer.

a Jeg ________ og leser.
b Hanne ________ og venter på trikken.
c Siri ________ til Helsinki neste mandag.
d ________ du og venter på meg?
e Katrine ________ på tyskkurs.

3 Describe your daily routine.

____

____

____

____

4 Rearrange the words into sentences; don't forget to place the capital letter on the first word.

a	vekker	deg	jeg	.					
b	jobben	langt	bor	jeg	fra	min	.		
c	å	liker	morgenen	lenge	sove	om	jeg	.	
d	skogen	tur	tar	etter	jeg	i	jobb	en	.
e	dusjer	jeg	,	først	frokost	spiser	så	jeg	.
f	meg	trenger	jeg	konsentrere	å	.			

SELF CHECK

	I CAN ...
○	... talk about the time.
○	... describe my daily routine.
○	... use reflexive verbs and reflexive pronouns.
○	... use some verbs of movement and adverbs of place.

R2 Review 2

4 Dette er familien min

1 Match the Norwegian with the English.

a bonusbarn	**1** stepmother
b svigerinne	**2** brother-in-law
c søster	**3** the father's mother
d mormor	**4** great-grandmother
e søsken	**5** niece
f farmor	**6** aunt
g niese	**7** sister-in-law
h tante	**8** grandfather
i onkel	**9** the mother's mother
j far	**10** sister
k oldemor	**11** uncle
l bestefar	**12** father
m stemor	**13** siblings
n svoger	**14** stepchild

2 Translate the following sentences into English.

a Hva betyr det?
b Hva heter «fiancé» på norsk?
c Det er veldig vanskelig å huske alt.
d Mammas søster heter Sigrid.
e Det blir koselig.

3 Translate the following sentences into Norwegian and say them out loud.

a My sister's name is Astrid.
b His stepbrother's name is Ciarán.
c His sister's name is Siobhán.
d Now I understand!
e What is the name of Tove's fiancé?
f What do you mean?

4 Fill in the blanks with the correct possessive pronoun.

- **a** _______ bror heter Martin. (*my*)
- **b** _______ søster heter Marianne. (*his*)
- **c** Guro og _______ mann bor i Spania. (*her*)
- **d** Kari er glad i barnet _______ . (*her own*)
- **e** Jeg kjører bilen _______ til verkstedet. (*your*, plural)
- **f** Han ringer vennen _______ . (*his own*)
- **g** Hun gifter seg med kjæresten _______ . (*her own*)
- **h** Kan du snakke med søstera _______ ? (*your*)

5 Complete the following crossword and find the mystery word.

1											
	2										
					3						
			4								
		5									
					6						
	7										
8											

Across:

What is the Norwegian for the following?

- **1** great-grandchild
- **2** father-in-law
- **3** son
- **4** daughter
- **5** uncle
- **6** mothers
- **7** great-great-grandfather
- **8** sister

Down:

Have you found the mystery word? What is it? _______

5 Vi skal handle!

1 Match the Norwegian with the English.

a	Han elsker henne.	**1**	The house is white.
b	Jeg har grønne sko på meg.	**2**	I hate wearing high-heeled shoes.
c	Bilen min er gul.	**3**	He loves her.
d	Denne kjolen er på tilbud.	**4**	I like you.
e	Huset er hvit.	**5**	A blue scarf.
f	Den nye lampa er fin.	**6**	She does not like me.
g	Et blått skjerf.	**7**	This dress is on sale.
h	Jeg hater høyhælte sko.	**8**	My car is yellow.
i	Jeg er glad i deg.	**9**	The new lamp is nice.
j	Hun liker meg ikke.	**10**	I am wearing green shoes.

2 Translate the following sentences into English.

a Jeg vil gjerne kjøpe en ny genser.
b Guro kan ikke komme i dag.
c Du bør lese norsk.
d Han skal til Roma neste sommer.
e Skal du kjøpe denne boka?
f Vil du treffe ham?
g Kan Frode hjelpe deg?
h Jeg må gå nå.
i Jeg bør gå nå.

3 Translate the following sentences into Norwegian and say them out loud.

a She is wearing blue shoes.
b I live in a small house.
c He has three small children.
d You have a red car.
e My friends are funny.
f This is a cosy room.

4 Match the adjective with the correct meaning.

a	**annerledes**	**1**	strange
b	**billig**	**2**	small
c	**dyr**	**3**	stylish / smart
d	**fantastisk**	**4**	quick
e	**flink**	**5**	old
f	**flott**	**6**	different
g	**gammel**	**7**	boring

h	**kjære**	**8**	funny
i	**kjedelig**	**9**	cheap
j	**koselig**	**10**	expensive
k	**liten**	**11**	fantastic
l	**morsom**	**12**	good at
m	**rar**	**13**	cosy
n	**rask**	**14**	dear
o	**stilig**	**15**	great

5 Complete the following crossword and find the mystery word.

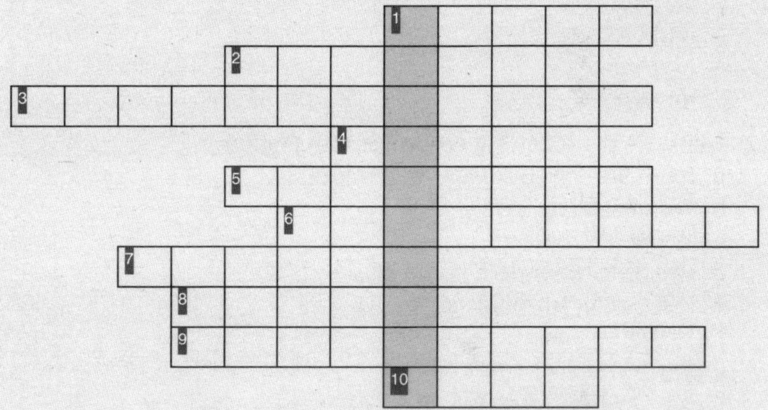

Across:

What is the Norwegian for the following?

1 trousers
2 shirt
3 tights
4 tie
5 underwear
6 swimsuit
7 sweater
8 mittens
9 miniskirt
10 sock

Down:

Have you found the mystery word? What is it? _______

6 Hva gjør du hver dag?

1 What time is it? Write the time, as in the example.

14.30 Klokka er / Den er halv tre.

- **a** 12.15
- **b** 17.45
- **c** 11.30
- **d** 10.10
- **e** 08.05
- **f** 16.20
- **g** 03.25
- **h** 06.40
- **i** 15.35

2 Translate the following sentences into English.

- **a** Jeg legger meg tidlig.
- **b** Jeg kommer for sent.
- **c** Jeg liker å sove lenge.
- **d** Hvor lang tid tar det?
- **e** Hva gjør du om morgenen?
- **f** Nesten en time.
- **g** Jeg må kjøpe en ny bil.
- **h** Etter jobb tar jeg en tur i skogen.
- **i** Vi kan treffes foran biblioteket.
- **j** Når er du ferdig?

3 Translate the following sentences into Norwegian and say them out loud.

- **a** I get up.
- **b** How long does it take?
- **c** Before breakfast, I take a shower.
- **d** I wake up.
- **e** I am wearing a hat.
- **f** I like sleeping until late.
- **g** I wear a jacket.
- **h** First, I take a shower, then I eat breakfast.

4 Fill in the blanks with the correct reflexive pronoun.

- **a** Han soler _______ .
- **b** Jeg tar på _______ jakka.
- **c** Jeg legger _______ tidlig.
- **d** Skynd _______ .
- **e** Hun liker _______ der.
- **f** Barnet ønsker _______ en hund.
- **g** Har du skjerf med _______ ?
- **h** De har ikke bestemt _______ .
- **i** Du må oppføre _______ pent.

5 Complete the following crossword.

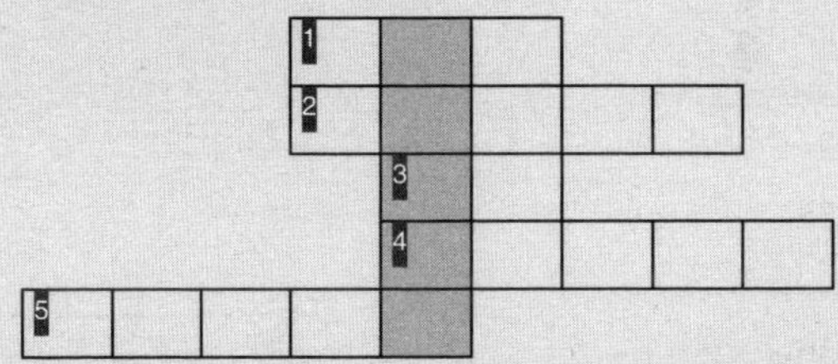

Across:

What is the Norwegian for the following?

- **1** (to) become / stay
- **2** (to) sit
- **3** (to) walk
- **4** (to) do
- **5** (to) come

Down:

Have you found the mystery word? What is it? _______

7

In this unit, you will learn how to:

- talk about and order food and drink at a restaurant.
- use the imperative form of verbs.
- use demonstrative pronouns.
- write a shopping list and follow a recipe.
- talk about food customs in Norway.

Vi skal ut og spise

My progress tracker

DAY / DATE	Listening	Speaking	Reading	Writing	Conversation
	○	○	○	○	○
	○	○	○	○	○
	○	○	○	○	○
	○	○	○	○	○
	○	○	○	○	○

Food customs in Norway

The Norwegian **klima** (*climate*) has heavily influenced Norwegian food customs. For this reason, **grønnsaker** (*vegetables*) were not a big part of the Norwegian **kosthold** (*diet*) until the 1700s, when **løk** (*onion*), **poteter** (*potatoes*), **bær** (*berries*) and **frukt** (*fruit*) were introduced. **Kjøtt** (*meat*) and **fisk** (*fish*), on the other hand, were very important, and they were salted and smoked to be preserved. **Melkeprodukter** (*milk products*) were widely consumed as well, but until the 1900s it was not common to drink **helmelk** (*whole milk*); instead, **myse** (*whey*), **smør** (*butter*) and **ost** (*cheese*) were very common. As well as using **kumelk** (*cow's milk*), it was also common **å lage** (*to make*) cheese with milk from **geiter** (*goats*), **sauer** (*sheep*) and **reinsdyr** (*reindeer*). A famous Norwegian goat cheese is **brunost** (*brown cheese*), made with **geitmelk** (*goat's milk*). Among the many **tradisjonelle matretter** (*traditional dishes*) there is **grøt** (similar to *porridge*), which can be **rømmegrøt** (*porridge with sour cream*), **havregrøt** (*oat pudding*) or **risgrøt** (similar to *rice pudding*). Then there are several recipes with fish, such as **laks** (*salmon*), **torsk** (*cod*), **sild** (*herring*), **makrell** (*mackerel*) and **ørret** (*trout*). A traditional Christmas fish dish is called **lutefisk** (*lye fish*). A very common fish dish often served in **karrisaus** (*curry sauce*) is the **fiskebolle** (*fishball*) or **fiskekake** (*fish cake*), which are actually fish dumplings, and often contain **reker** (*shrimps*) or **skalldyr** (*crustaceans*). Some traditional meat dishes include **lammestek** (*lamb roast*), **pinnekjøtt** (*lamb or mutton roast*), **juleribbe** (*pork roast*, eaten at Christmas), **lapskaus** (*beef stew*), **elgkarbonader**, **kjøttkaker** or **kjøttboller** (*meat dumplings / meatballs*). Depending on the season, there are also many different kinds of desserts and sweets available, such as **kanelbolle** (*cinnamon bun*), **rosinbolle** (*raisin bun*), **lussekatt** (*saffron bun*), **pannekake** (*pancake*), **vaffel** (*waffle*), **bløtkake** (*cream cake*), and **kransekake** (*crown cake*). Norwegians love **is** (*ice cream*) and especially **softis** (*soft serve*). **Barn** (*children*) and **voksne** (*adults*) usually eat both **is** and **pølser** (*sausages*) on the 17th of May, after the parade. On the 17th of May, Constitution Day, people wear traditional Norwegian costumes, and children and students march in the main streets playing instruments, carrying the Norwegian flag and singing the national anthem.

What do you think elgkarbonader means in English?

Vocabulary builder

07.01 Listen to the following words related to food, and then repeat, trying to imitate the Norwegian pronunciation. Then complete with the missing translations in English.

FRUKT	______
banan	______
druer	*grapes*
eple	______
pære	*pear*
vannmelon	*watermelon*
fersken	*peach*
aprikos	______
kirsebær	*cherry*
jordbær	*strawberry*
blåbær	______

bringebær	*raspberry*
bjørnebær	*blackberry*
tyttebær	*lingonberry*
multe	*cloudberry*

GRØNNSAKER	**VEGETABLES**
agurk	*cucumber*
artisjokk	*artichoke*
aubergine	________
fennikel	*fennel*
gulrot	*carrot*
potet	________
spinat	________
squash	________
tomat	________

DRIKKE	________
juice	________
melk	________
øl	*beer*
vann	*water*
vin	________

NEW EXPRESSIONS

Some of these new expressions are used in the following dialogues. Note their meaning and the differences between the various alternatives.

Smaker det godt?	*Does it taste good?*
Jeg synes det i hvert fall.	*At least in my opinion.*
Du får bestemme selv.	*You can decide for yourself.*
Dette er gøy!	*This is fun!*
Ja, selvfølgelig!	*Yes, sure!*
Hva skal det være?	*What would you like?*
Hva slags vil du ha?	*What type would you like?*
Vil du ha noe annet?	*Do you want anything else?*
Vil du ha noe å drikke?	*Would you like something to drink? (lit. Do you want something to drink?)*
Vil du bestille?	*Do you want to order?*
Er du klar til å bestille?	*Are you ready to order?*
Hva vil du spise?	*lit. What do you want to eat?*
Hva vil du drikke?	*lit. What do you want to drink?*

Dialogue 1

07.02 *Camilla needs to buy some bread and pastries. She goes to the bakery, and then decides to order something to eat and drink as well. Listen carefully to the dialogue before answering the questions.*

1 Is Camilla in a hurry?

2 What is Camilla allergic to?

Bakeren	Hei, hva skal det være?
Camilla	Hei, jeg vil gjerne ha noen rundstykker, takk.
Bakeren	Hva slags vil du ha?
Camilla	To grovbrødrundstykker og to lyse, takk.
Bakeren	To grove og to lyse, her er de, har du prøvd sesamrundstykkene våre?
Camilla	Nei, jeg er allergisk mot sesamfrø.
Bakeren	Skjønner. Vil du ha noe annet?
Camilla	Ja takk, jeg tar et stykke eplekake og et stykke gulrotkake. Er det nøtter i gulrotkaken?
Bakeren	Ikke i oppskriften, men det kan være spor.
Camilla	Det går bra, jeg er ikke veldig allergisk mot nøtter.
Bakeren	Ok, vil du ha noe annet?
Camilla	Ja, jeg tar to hveteboller og to rosinboller. Og så en skolebolle.
Bakeren	Ok, skal du ta med alt eller spiser du noe her?
Camilla	Jeg tar alt med... Nei, jeg er egentlig sulten, så jeg tror jeg skal også ta et smørbrød med laks og egg.
Bakeren	Noe å drikke?
Camilla	Ja, appelsinjuice og en kopp kaffe, takk.
Bakeren	Da blir det 259 kroner til sammen.

3 Read the dialogue again and answer the questions.

- **a** How much bread does she buy?
- **b** What kind of cakes does she buy?
- **c** Which buns does she buy?
- **d** What does she decide to eat?
- **e** What does she drink?
- **f** How much does she pay?

4 Look at the conversation again, then match the Norwegian with the English translation.

a Hva skal det være?
b Vil du ha noe annet?
c Det kan være spor.
d Spiser du noe her?
e Jeg tar alt med.
f Jeg er egentlig sulten.

1 I'm actually hungry.
2 Are you going to eat anything here?
3 Do you want anything else?
4 There can be traces.
5 What can I do for you?
6 I'm taking everything away.

5 How do Camilla and the baker say the following?

a hungry
  1 jeg er allergisk mot **2** til sammen
  3 noe annet **4** sulten

b something else
  1 jeg er allergisk mot **2** til sammen
  3 noe annet **4** sulten

c I'm allergic to
  1 jeg er allergisk mot **2** til sammen
  3 noe annet **4** sulten

d altogether
  1 jeg er allergisk mot **2** til sammen
  3 noe annet **4** sulten

Language discovery 1

DEMONSTRATIVE PRONOUNS

Study the following table.

Entall – *singular*				Flertall – *plural*	
Hankjønn – *masculine* / hunkjønn – *feminine*		Intetkjønn – *neuter*		Hankjønn – *masculine* / hunkjønn – *feminine* / intetkjønn – *neuter*	
denne	*this (m / f)*	**dette**	*this (n)*	**disse**	*these*
den	*that (m / f)*	**det**	*that (n)*	**de**	*those*

1 Match the Norwegian with the English translation.

a Denne kaka er god.
b Denne mannen heter Lars.
c Dette barnet heter Hans.

1 That table is new.
2 That cake is good.
3 That child's name is Olav.

d	Dette er min venn Marius.	**4**	This man's name is Lars.
e	Disse glassene er ikke rene.	**5**	This child's name is Hans.
f	Det bordet der er nytt.	**6**	This cake is good.
g	Den kaka er god.	**7**	This is my friend Marius.
h	Det barnet heter Olav.	**8**	These glasses are not clean.
i	De rundstykkene er ferske.	**9**	Is this bread fresh?
j	Er det hasselnøtter i denne kaka?	**10**	Those rolls are freshly baked.
k	Er dette brødet ferskt?	**11**	Are there any hazelnuts in this cake?

Dialogue 2

07.03 *Thorbjørn and his English friend Cyan are going to cook* ***lapskaus****, a typical Norwegian dish, but they need to buy ingredients. Listen carefully to the dialogue before answering the questions.*

1 Has Cyan tried lapskaus before?

2 Do they need to buy all the ingredients in the recipe?

Thorbjørn	Så du vet ikke hva lapskaus er.
Cyan	Nei, smaker det godt?
Thorbjørn	Ja, jeg synes det i hvert fall, men du får bestemme selv når du smaker den.
Cyan	Ok, dette er gøy! Hva trenger vi?
Thorbjørn	Jeg vet ikke, la meg se på nettet først.
Cyan	Finnes det en side med tradisjonelle norske oppskrifter?
Thorbjørn	Ja, selvfølgelig, den heter MatPrat.
Cyan	Å, smart navn!
Thorbjørn	Ok, så vi trenger storfekjøtt, smør, buljong, poteter, gulrøtter, kålrot, persillerot, salt og pepper. Kan du skrive en liste?
Cyan	Ja, storfekjøtt, pepper ...
Thorbjørn	Nei, jeg har masse pepper, og jeg har også buljong, smør og poteter.
Cyan	Ok, så storfekjøtt, gulrøtter, kålrot og persillerot. Har du salt?
Thorbjørn	Ja, det har jeg også.

LAPSKAUS

INGREDIENSER:

600 g storfekjøtt av høyrygg eller bog, uten bein
2 ss smør, til steking
4 dl vann
1 stk buljongterning
6 stk potet, i terninger
3 stk gulrot, i terninger
1 skive kålrot, i terninger
1 stk persillerot, i terninger
1 ts salt
1/2 ts grovmalt pepper

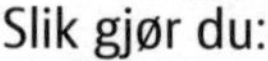

Slik gjør du:

1. Skjær kjøtt i terninger. Ha smør i en varm stekepanne. Vent til smøret slutter å bruse, og brun kjøttet i små porsjoner.
2. Ha kjøttet i en gryte, hell over vann og ha i buljongterning. Tilsett potet- og grønnsaksterninger, og la det småkoke på middels varme til grønnsakene er godt møre.
3. Rør minst mulig slik at lapskausen ikke blir grøtet, men se til at den ikke svir seg i bunnen. Smak til med salt og pepper.
4. Server med grovt brød eller flatbrød og tyttebær.

3 Read the dialogue again and answer the questions.

a Which ingredients do they need to buy?
b Which ingredients do they already have?
c Does Thorbjørn like *lapskaus*?
d What is the name of the website where they found the recipe?
e What does it mean?

4 Look at the conversation again, then match the Norwegian with the English translation.

a Fordi jeg må kjøpe en ny bil først.
b Du får bestemme selv når du smaker den.
c Finnes det en side med tradisjonelle norske oppskrifter?
d Jeg har masse pepper.

1 Is there a website with traditional Norwegian recipes?
2 At least in my opinion.
3 I have lots of pepper.
4 You can decide for yourself when you have tasted it.

5 What words do Cyan and Thorbjørn use to say the following?

a surely
- **1** tradisjonelle
- **2** oppskrifter
- **3** selvfølgelig
- **4** smart

b amusing / funny
- **1** gøy
- **2** først
- **3** selvfølgelig
- **4** smart

c is there
- **1** gøy
- **2** først
- **3** finnes det
- **4** tradisjonelle

d firstly
- **1** gøy
- **2** først
- **3** selvfølgelig
- **4** smart

e traditional
- **1** først
- **2** tradisjonelle
- **3** oppskrifter
- **4** selvfølgelig

f recipes
- **1** først
- **2** tradisjonelle
- **3** oppskrifter
- **4** selvfølgelig

g clever
- **1** tradisjonelle
- **2** oppskrifter
- **3** selvfølgelig
- **4** smart

6 Choose the correct translation for each of the following expressions.

a I don't know.
  1 Smaker den godt?
  2 Hva trenger vi?
  3 Jeg vet ikke.
  4 Kan du skrive ei liste?

b What do we need?
  1 Smaker den godt?
  2 Hva trenger vi?
  3 Jeg vet ikke.
  4 Kan du skrive ei liste?

c Can you write a list?
  1 Smaker den godt?
  2 Hva trenger vi?
  3 Jeg vet ikke.
  4 Kan du skrive ei liste?

d Does it taste good?
  1 Smaker den godt?
  2 Hva trenger vi?
  3 Jeg vet ikke.
  4 Kan du skrive ei liste?

7 What do you think the following abbreviations mean? Choose the correct alternative.

a stk
  1 piece
  2 teaspoon
  3 tablespoon

b ss
  1 piece
  2 teaspoon
  3 tablespoon

c ts
  1 piece
  2 teaspoon
  3 tablespoon

CULTURE TIP

Fårikål (*Norwegian mutton* or *lamb and cabbage stew*) is considered by many to be Norway's national dish. It is eaten during the autumn months, when cabbage is in season, and has its own day (**fårikålens dag**) on the last Thursday in September. **Fårikål** consists of few ingredients and is quite easy to make.
However, there are at least two dishes that are definitely more popular: **Pizza Grandiosa**, of which Norwegians consume around 50 million a year, and tacos. **Tacofredag** (*Friday tacos*) has been a staple for Norwegian families since the 1990s when Mexican cuisine became popular.

Recipe for fårikål

Language discovery 2

IMPERATIVE FORM

To give orders and directions, for example in a recipe, we use the imperative form of the verb. Look at the following examples:

Å gå	**Gå!**	*Go!*
Å snakke	**Snakk!**	*Speak!*
Å komme	**Kom!**	*Come!*

1 Look at the following infinitives and choose the correct imperative form.

a å gjøre
  1 gjør
  2 gjøre

b å se
  1 se
  2 ser

c å gå
  1 gå
  2 går

d å snakke
  1 snak
  2 snakk

e å komme
  1 kom
  2 komm

f å sove
  1 sove
  2 sov

g å høre
  1 hør
  2 høre

h å lese
  1 les
  2 leser

2 **Look at the following examples taken from the recipe in Dialogue 2 and turn the imperatives into infinitives.**

a	**Skjær** kjøtt i terninger.	*Cut the meat in cubes.*
b	**Ha** smør i en varm stekepanne.	*Put (lit. have) the butter in a frying pan.*
c	**Vent** til smøret slutter å bruse.	*Wait until the butter stops spitting.*
d	**Brun** kjøttet i små porsjoner.	*Brown the meat in small portions.*
e	**Hell** over vann.	*Pour water over.*
f	**Tilsett** potet.	*Add potatoes.*
g	**La** det småkoke.	*Let it simmer.*
h	**Rør** minst mulig.	*Stir as little as possible.*
i	**Se** til at den ikke svir seg i bunnen.	*Check that it isn't burned at the bottom.*
j	**Smak** til med salt og pepper.	*Add salt and pepper to taste.*
k	**Server** med grovt brød.	*Serve with wholemeal bread.*

3 **Choose from the alternatives to fill in the blanks with the correct form of the imperative.**

a _______ hit nå!
1 komme
2 komm
3 kom

b _______ norsk, vær så snill!
1 snakk
2 å snakke
3 snakke

c _______ hjem med én gang!
1 å gå
2 gå
3 går

d _______ boka!
1 lese
2 å lese
3 les

e _______ det til meg!
1 å si
2 sier
3 si

f _______ det nå!
1 gjøre
2 å gjøre
3 gjør

g _______ med meg!
1 å danse
2 dans
3 danse

h _______ å bråke!
1 slutte
2 slutt
3 å slutte

Practice

1 07.04 Listening and speaking

Listen to the following recipe, and then read it aloud.

LAPPER MED BLÅBÆR OG KREM

INGREDIENSER:

3 ss smør
4 dl hvetemel
3 dl melk
5 egg
½ dl sukker
½ ts salt
1 ts bakepulver
3 dl kremfløte
ca. 2 dl blåbærsyltetøy

Slik gjør du:

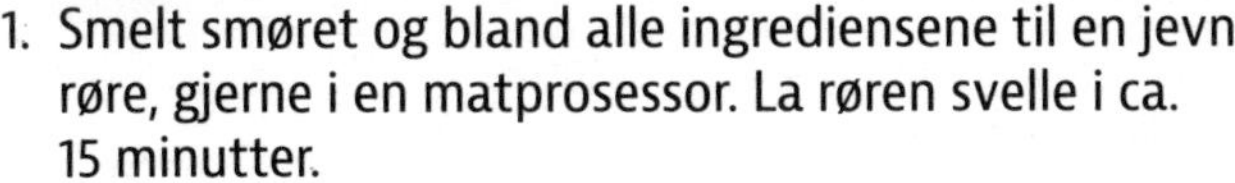

1. Smelt smøret og bland alle ingrediensene til en jevn røre, gjerne i en matprosessor. La røren svelle i ca. 15 minutter.
2. Stek lappene i litt smør i varm stekepanne. Snu dem når røren er stivnet på overflaten.
3. Server lappene lune med pisket kremfløte og blåbærsyltetøy.

Tips: Rislapper smaker også kjempegodt! Rør inn rester av risgrøt i lapperøren. Spe eventuelt med litt melk dersom røren blir tykk.

The word **tips** means *suggestion*, and it is singular, even if it ends with an **-s**.

2 Hannah is at the library where she writes an email to her girlfriend Iselin to plan their evening. Read her email and answer the questions.

New message

Fra: Hannah
Dato: 3. mars 2025
Til: Iselin
Objekt: Middag i kveld

Hei elskling,

Jeg tar meg en liten pause for a planlegge kvelden. Jeg vil gjerne bestille et bord pa restaurant klokka 18, sa vi rekker konserten klokka 22.

Har du lyst til a spise noe spesielt? Jeg har litt lyst pa indisk mat, men meksikansk frister ogsa, hva synes du?

Nar kommer Frode og Lasse? Spiser de med oss? Jeg husker ikke.

Jeg gleder meg til i kveld!

Klem
Hannah

- **a** When does she want to book the table?
- **b** When is the concert?
- **c** What would she like to eat?
- **d** Does she remember whether Frode and Lasse are going to eat with them?

3 How does Hannah say the following?

- **a** I'm looking forward to tonight!
- **b** Mexican food is appealing.
- **c** I'm taking a break to plan the evening.

LANGUAGE TIP

If you are a vegetarian or a vegan, in Norwegian you can say **Jeg er vegetarianer** or **Jeg er veganer**.

Test yourself

1 Write a shopping list of things you need to buy at the grocery store today.

____

____

____

____

2 Rearrange the words into sentences; don't forget to place the capital letter on the first word.

a bestille vil bord gjerne restaurant jeg et på .
b klokka vi konserten rekker 22 ?
c har indisk litt jeg på lyst mat .
d synes du hva ?
e de spiser oss med ?
f til gleder kveld meg jeg i !

3 Write a short recipe for a simple dish you like. Don't forget quantities and ingredients.

4 How would you do the following?

a order meatballs with mashed peas, potatoes, brown sauce, lingonberry jam and a beer
b order a cinnamon bun, a glass of cold milk and a cup of coffee
c list your allergies
d tell someone that you're vegetarian

SELF CHECK

	I CAN ...
●	... order a meal.
●	... say what food I like and dislike.
●	... follow a recipe.
●	... give short directions.

8

In this unit, you will learn how to:
» book a hotel room, plan a journey and buy tickets.
» ask for, follow and give directions.
» talk about dates and time.
» use ordinal numbers.
» talk about health and illnesses and refer to different body parts.

På ferie i Norge

My progress tracker

DAY / DATE					
	○	○	○	○	○
	○	○	○	○	○
	○	○	○	○	○
	○	○	○	○	○
	○	○	○	○	○

Tourist attractions in Norway

Norway is without any doubt **et vakkert land** (*a beautiful country*), and for a **turist** (*tourist*), there are plenty of activities to do and places to visit. If you are interested in sport, you can **sykle** (*cycle*), **gå på ski** (*ski*), or **spille golf** (*play golf*). If you are more adventurous, you can **klatre** (*hike*), **dykke** (*scuba-dive*), or **prøve** (*try*) **rafting**, kiting, **snøkiting** snow-kiting, **paragliding**, **fallskjermhopping** (*parachuting*) and **isklatring** (*ice climbing*), and even take a **grottetur** (*caving trip*) or a **fisketur** (*fishing trip*). If you want to be in close contact with nature, you can try **hundekjøring** (*dog sledding*), **rideturer** (*horse-riding tours*), **reinkjøring** (*reindeer sledding*), take a **kano-** (*canoe*) or **kajakktur** (*kayak trip*), or even a **hvalsafari** (*whale safari*). If you are more interested in **museer** (*museums*) and **gallerier** (*galleries*), in Norway you will find these almost everywhere, as well as **monumenter** (*monuments*). Furthermore, Norway houses eight **steder** (*places*) featured in **UNESCOs verdensarvliste** (*UNESCO World Heritage Sites*).

Last but not least, Norway also offers stunning nature, with its **fjorder** (*fjords*), **fjell** (*mountains*), **nasjonalparker** (*national parks*), **fosser** (*waterfalls*), **øyer** (*isles*), **isbreer** (*glaciers*), **strender** (*seaside*), and, obviously, **midnattsol** (*midnight sun*) during the summer and **nordlys** (*Northern Lights*) during the winter. In Norway you can also **overnatte** (*stay overnight*) in a **hotell** (*hotel*), B&B, **vandrerhjem** (*youth hostel*), **hytte** (*cottage*), **leilighet** (*apartment*), or even an entire **hus** (*house*). Otherwise, and especially if you like **å reise grønt** (*green traveling*), you can go camping, stay in a **fyr** (*lighthouse*), or even at a **gård** (*farm*). If you **planlegger** (*are planning*) **ferien** (*a holiday*) in Norway, a very useful website is www.visitnorway.com. When you want to **bestille** (*book*) a **rom** (*room*) or a **billett** (*ticket*) for a **buss** (*bus*), **tog** (*train*) or **fly** (*plane*), you can use **appen** (*the app*) or **bestille på nettet** (*order/book online*).

What does vandrerhjem mean?

Vocabulary builder

08.01 **Listen to the following ordinal numbers, and then repeat, trying to imitate the Norwegian pronunciation.**

NUMBERS (1ST–21ST)

første	*1st*	tolvte	*12th*
andre	*2nd*	trettende	*13th*
tredje	*3rd*	fjortende	*14th*
fjerde	*4th*	femtende	*15th*
femte	*5th*	sekstende	*16th*
sjette	*6th*	syttende	*17th*
sjuende	*7th*	attende	*18th*
åttende	*8th*	nittende	*19th*
niende	*9th*	tjuende	*20th*
tiende	*10th*	tjueførste	*21st*
ellevte	*11th*		

LANGUAGE TIP

When writing ordinals as numbers, remember to include the full stop .

1\. (første) 2. (andre) 3. (tredje)

etc.

NUMBERS (TENS AND HUNDREDS)

trettiende	*30th*
førtiende	*40th*
femtiende	*50th*
sekstiende	*60th*
syttiende	*70th*
åttiende	*80th*
nittiende	*90th*
hundrede	*100th*
hundrede og en	*101st*
tohundrede	*200th*
trehundrede	*300th*
firehundrede og femtisjette	*456th*
tusende	*1,000th*
sju / syvtusende	*7,000th*
titusende	*10,000th*

LANGUAGE TIP

13.11.2025 **trettende i ellevte, to tusen og tjuefem.**

As you can see from the example, in Norwegian the date is given with a full stop, the order is always day, month, then year and when we read it, we have to use ordinal numbers for both the day and the month. As in English, when we talk about dates we always have to use **den** (*the*) before the ordinal number.

Hvilken dato er det i dag? I dag er den 17. mai.
What date is it today? Today is the 17th of May.

NEW EXPRESSIONS

Some of these new expressions are used in the following dialogues. Note their meaning and the differences between the various alternatives.

Hvor ligger museet?	*Where is the museum?*
Hvor ligger sykehuset?	*Where is the hospital?*
Vær så snill.	*Please.*
Kunne / Kan du hjelpe meg?	*Could / Can you help me?*
Jeg føler meg dårlig.	*I feel bad.*
Jeg er syk.	*I am ill.*
Jeg er kvalm/uvel.	*I feel sick.*
Jeg har vondt i magen.	*I have a bellyache. (lit. I have a pain in the belly.)*
Jeg har vondt i ryggen.	*I have a backache.*

Jeg har vondt i hodet.	*I have a headache. (lit. I have a pain in the head.)*
Jeg har hodepine.	*I have a headache.*
Jeg har vondt i halsen.	*I have a sore throat. (lit. I have a pain in my throat.)*
Jeg er forkjølet.	*I have a cold.*
Jeg har feber.	*I have a fever.*
Ta til venstre.	*Turn left.*
Ta til høyre.	*Turn right.*
Gå rett fram.	*Go straight ahead.*
Følg veien.	*Follow the street.*

Dialogue 1

08.02 *Marion and Andrew are visiting Bergen for the first time and they want to visit the aquarium. Their phones are out of power, so they have to use a map and ask for directions. Listen carefully to the dialogue before answering the questions.*

1 Do they live far from the aquarium?

2 Is it raining today?

Marion	Vi vil gjerne se akvariet i dag, er det langt borte?
Gunnar	Nei, dere kan gå dit, det tar ti, femten minutter, har du kart? Jeg kan vise dere hvor dere må gå.
Marion	Ja, her er kartet.
Gunnar	Takk. Ok, så vi er her, i Lille Markeveien. Herifra må dere gå 100 meter langs Lille Markeveien mot nord, så tar dere til venstre og går 20 meter, etterpå tar dere veien til høyre, den heter Klosteret. Etter 200 meter tar dere til venstre i Ytre Markeveien. Etter 100 meter tar dere til høyre, og etter 15 meter går dere rett fram, dere følger veien i 500 meter og finner akvariet.
Andrew	Takk, Jeg er sikker på at vi finner det! Hva synes du vi bør se etter akvariet?
Gunnar	Dere må se Bryggen, og så kan dere gå til Bergenhus Festning. Og så ta dere en tur i området, det er fullt av museer, restauranter og butikker, det er også julehuset, det vil dere sikkert like.

Andrew	Å, ja! Jeg vil gjerne se julehuset!
Gunnar	Og så kan dere ta Fløibanen og se hele byen.
Marion	Det vil jeg absolutt gjøre, men det regner i dag, det er best å vente til i morgen, når det er meldt sol.
Gunnar	Ja, jeg er enig, det er en god idé.
Marion	Og så vil jeg gjerne se Fisketorget, hvor ligger det?
Gunnar	Det ligger i Strandkaien, ved siden av turistinformasjon.
Marion	Å, ja, nå husker jeg. Tusen takk!
Gunnar	Bare hyggelig, ha en fin dag.
Andrew	Takk, i like måte.

3 Re-read the dialogue and answer the following questions.

a Where does Gunnar say they should go after the aquarium?
b Where does Gunnar say they could eat?
c What does Gunnar say they would enjoy visiting?
d What else do they decide to visit?
e When do they decide to take the Fløibanen funicular?

4 Look at the conversation again, then match the Norwegian with the English translation.

a Er det langt borte?
b Jeg kan vise dere hvor dere må gå.
c Hva synes du vi bør se?
d Det vil dere sikkert like.
e Det vil jeg absolutt gjøre!
f Det er best å vente til i morgen, når det er meldt sol.

1 It's better to wait until tomorrow, when the forecast is sunny.
2 I absolutely want to do that!
3 Is it far from here?
4 What do you think we should see?
5 I can show you where you have to go.
6 You will certainly like that.

5 How do Gunnar, Marion and Andrew say the following?

a take the road to the left
1 ta en tur i området
2 gå rett fram
3 ta til venstre
4 ta til høyre

b take the road to the right
1 ta en tur i området
2 gå rett fram
3 ta til venstre
4 ta til høyre

c from here
1. herifra
2. ta en tur i området
3. gå rett fram
4. ta til venstre

d take a walk in the area
1. herifra
2. ta en tur i området
3. gå rett fram
4. i like måte

e likewise
1. gå rett fram
2. ta til venstre
3. ta til høyre
4. i like måte

f go straight ahead
1. gå rett fram
2. ta til venstre
3. ta til høyre
4. i like måte

Language discovery

PREPOSITIONS OF PLACE

In Norwegian there are many prepositions; here we are going to focus on some prepositions of place. Look at the following table and try to memorize the different prepositions.

Norwegian	*English*
Ved siden av	*Beside*
Fiskemarkedet ligger *ved siden av* turistinformasjon. **Suvenirbutikken ligger *ved siden av* postkontoret.**	*The fish market is beside the tourist information office.* *The souvenir shop is beside the post office.*
I nærheten av	*In the vicinity of*
Restauranten er *i nærheten av* Bryggen. **Vi bor *i nærheten av* museet.**	*The restaurant is in the vicinity of Bryggen.* *We live in the vicinity of the museum.*
Til venstre (for)	*To the left*
Postkontoret ligger *til venstre for* banken. **Da tar dere *til venstre.***	*The post office is to the left of the bank.* *Then you turn to the left.*
Til høyre (for)	*To the right*
Banken ligger *til høyre for* postkontoret. **Så tar dere veien *til høyre.***	*The bank is to the right of the post office.* *Then you take the street on the right.*
Rett fram	*Straight ahead*
Etter 15 meter går dere *rett fram.*	*After 15 meters you walk straight ahead.*
Utenfor	*Outside of*
Jeg står *utenfor* kirka.	*I'm standing outside of the church.*

Foran	*In front of*
Banken og postkontoret ligger *foran* kjøpesenteret. **Hun sitter *foran* meg på bussen.**	*The bank and the post office are in front of the shopping center.* *She's sitting in front of me on the bus.*
Bak	*Behind*
Hun sitter *bak* meg på bussen. **Katten gjemmer seg *bak* sofaen.**	*She's sitting behind me on the bus.* *The cat is hiding behind the sofa.*
Mellom	*Between*
Butikken ligger *mellom* postkontoret og skolen. **Sverige ligger *mellom* Norge og Finland.**	*The shop is between the post office and the school.* *Sweden is between Norway and Finland.*
Blant	*Among*
Hun liker å være *blant* sine venner.	*She likes being among her friends.*
Over	*Over*
Lampa henger *over* senga. **Skiltet henger *over* døra.**	*The lamp is hanging over the bed.* *The sign is hanging over the door.*
Under	*Under*
Hunden ligger *under* bordet. **Jeg sover *under* dyna.**	*The dog is lying under the table.* *I'm sleeping under the duvet.*

1 Fill in the blanks with the correct preposition.

a Da tar dere ________. (*to the left*)
b Da tar dere ________. (*to the right*)
c Etter 15 meter går dere ________ i Nordnesveien. (*straight ahead*)
d Hun liker å være ________ sine venner. (*among*)
e Hun sitter ________ meg på bussen. (*behind*)
f Hun sitter ________ meg på bussen. (*in front of*)
g Hunden ligger ________ bordet. (*under*)
h Jeg står ________ kirka. (*outside of*)
i Lampa henger ________ senga. (*over*)
j Suvenirbutikken ligger ________ postkontoret. (*beside*)
k Suvenirbutikken ligger ________ postkontoret. (*in the vicinity of*)
l Suvenirbutikken ligger ________ postkontoret. (*to the left*)
m Suvenirbutikken ligger ________ postkontoret. (*to the right*)
n Sverige ligger ________ Norge og Finland. (*between*)

Dialogue 2

08.03 *Maja and Mathias are going to take their Canadian friend Angelica to the souvenir shop to buy presents for her friends and family back home, when they realize they still need to buy train tickets for the following day. Listen carefully to the dialogue before answering the questions.*

1 What does Angelica want to buy?

2 Where are they going to before the souvenir shop?

Angelica	Jeg vil gjerne kjøpe gaver til venner og familien, og så trenger jeg kort.
Maja	Vi kan gå til suvenirbutikken i sentrum. Hva trenger du å kjøpe?
Angelica	Jeg trenger femten kort, og så noe norsk å ta med hjem.
Mathias	Vi må også kjøpe togbilletter til i morgen, det er lurt å gjøre det med én gang. Vi kan kjøpe dem på reisebyrå og så gå til suvenirbutikken som ligger ved siden av postkontoret.
Angelica	Det høres bra ut.
På reisebyrå ...	
Selgeren	Hei, hva kan jeg hjelpe dere med?
Maja	Hei, vi trenger å bestille togbilletter til Lillehammer.
Selgeren	Hvor mange trenger dere og når vil dere reise?
Maja	Vi er tre og vi vil gjerne reise tidlig i morgen.
Selgeren	Trenger dere tur-retur?
Maja	Ja, takk. Vi tenker å reise tilbake sent på søndag.
Selgeren	Det blir 1494 kroner til sammen. Toget går på fredag kl. 7 og dere kommer tilbake på søndag kl. 22.
Maja	Fantastisk! Kan du bestille overnatting også?
Selgeren	Selvfølgelig. Hvor vil dere bo? Skal jeg se etter et dobbeltrom og et enkeltrom?
Maja	Vi har ikke råd til noe kjempedyrt. Så et tremannsrom kan være fint.
Selgeren	Jeg ser på vandrerhjemmet først da... ja, de har et tremannsrom ledig til 2190 kroner inkludert frokost.
Maja	Fantastisk, vi tar det. Er wifi gratis?
Selgeren	Ja, det er det.
Maja	Supert! Kan jeg betale med kort?
Selgeren	Ja, det kan du.

3 Re-read the dialogue and answer the following questions.

- **a** Where is the souvenir shop?
- **b** What is next to it?
- **c** How many postcards does Angelica need?
- **d** How much do the tickets cost?
- **e** What kind of room do they book?
- **f** How much does it cost?
- **g** How long are they staying?

4 Look at the conversation again, then match the Norwegian with the English translation.

- **a** Det høres bra ut.
- **b** Jeg trenger femten kort, og så noe norsk å ta med hjem.
- **c** Hei, hva kan jeg hjelpe dere med?
- **d** Hvor mange trenger dere og når vil dere reise?
- **e** Kan du bestille overnatting også?
- **f** Skal jeg se etter et dobbeltrom og et enkeltrom?
- **g** Vi har ikke råd til noe kjempedyrt.

1. Hi, what can I help you with?
2. We cannot afford anything really expensive.
3. Can you book overnight accommodation as well?
4. Shall I look for a double and a single room?
5. I need 15 postcards, and then something Norwegian to take home.
6. How many do you need and when do you want to travel?
7. Sounds good.

5 How do the people in the dialogue say the following?

a fantastic
1 gjerne **2** fantastisk **3** supert

b wonderful
1 gjerne **2** fantastisk **3** supert

c to book
1 gjerne **2** bestille **3** betale

d to pay
1 gjerne **2** bestille **3** betale

e gladly
1 gjerne **2** fantastisk **3** supert

f double room
1 dobbeltrom **2** enkeltrom **3** tremannsrom

g single room
  1 dobbeltrom **2** enkeltrom **3** tremannsrom

h triple room
  1 dobbeltrom **2** enkeltrom **3** tremannsrom

i return ticket
  1 tur-retur **2** bestille **3** betale

LANGUAGE AND CULTURE TIP

If you have a **funksjonsnedsettelse** (*disability*) you might need to check for accessibility. If you are a **rullestolbruker** (*wheelchair user*) you might want to be able to ask if there is a **rampe** (*ramp*) or a **heis** (*elevator*) in the **hotell** (*hotel*) you are booking. Recently a campaign has been launched in Norway: **«Ikke alle funksjonsnedsettelser er synlige»** (*not all disabilities are visible*). To make public toilets more **inkluderende** (*inclusive*) toward people with **usynlige funksjonsnedsettelser** (*invisible disabilities*) such as **diabetes**, **fatigue**, **kreft** (*cancer*), **ME** (*Myalgic Encephalomyelitis*), **osv.** (*etc.*), the illustration of a wheelchair user on toilet doors has been changed to include a man and a woman also.

Practice

1 08.04 **Listen to the second part of the previous dialogue again and fill in the blanks.**

På ________

Selgeren	Hei, hva kan jeg ________ dere med?
Maja	Hei, vi trenger å ________ togbilletter til Lillehammer.
Selgeren	Hvor mange trenger dere og når vil dere ________?
Maja	Vi er tre og vi vil ________ reise tidlig i morgen.
Selgeren	Trenger dere ________?
Maja	Ja, takk. Vi tenker å reise tilbake sent på søndag.
Selgeren	Det blir 1494 kroner til sammen. Toget går på fredag kl. 7 og dere kommer tilbake på søndag kl. 22.
Maja	Fantastisk! Kan du bestille ________ også?
Selgeren	Selvfølgelig. Hvor vil dere bo? Skal jeg se etter et ________ og et ________?

Maja	Vi har ikke råd til noe kjempedyrt. Så et ________ kan være fint.
Selgeren	Jeg ser på ________ først da ... ja, de har et ________ ledig til 2190 kroner ________ frokost.
Maja	Fantastisk, vi tar det. Er wifi gratis?
Selgeren	Ja, det er det.
Maja	Supert! Kan jeg ________ med kort?
Selgeren	Ja, det kan du.

2 Ritesh and Olivia are on holiday in Norway but Ritesh is not feeling too well and they decide to visit a doctor at the legevakta. Read the following description of Ritesh's symptoms and answer the questions.

Jeg føler meg svak, jeg fryser og har vondt overalt. Jeg tror jeg har feber, og så har jeg veldig vondt både i ryggen og i nakken. I tillegg er jeg kvalm og har mistet matlysten. Jeg nyser hele tiden og har begynt å hoste. Og ja, jeg har også vondt i halsen.

- **a** How does Ritesh feel?
- **b** Where does it hurt?
- **c** Does he have a fever?

3 How does Ritesh say the following? Match the Norwegian with the English translation.

a Jeg nyser hele tiden.	**1** I'm cold.
b Jeg er kvalm.	**2** I'm feeling weak.
c Jeg føler meg svak.	**3** I think I have a fever.
d Jeg fryser.	**4** I'm nauseous.
e Jeg har begynt å hoste.	**5** I sneeze all the time.
f Jeg tror jeg har feber.	**6** I have begun coughing.

Test yourself

1 Imagine you are unwell. Describe how you are feeling and what parts of your body are aching.

2 Rearrange the words into sentences; don't forget to place the capital letter on the first word.

a	må	mot	gå	nord	langs	dere	herifra	veien	.
b	da	til	venstre	dere	tar	.			
c	til	så	tar	høyre	dere	veien	.		
d	dere	meter	etter	venstre	tar	200	til		.
e	meter	100	tar	etter	til	dere	høyre		.
f	15	rett	går	meter	etter	fram	dere		.

3 Write a short text addressed to a friend, in which you explain to them how to reach your home from the city center.

___

___

___

___

4 When is your birthday? Write the complete date.

___

___

SELF CHECK

	I CAN ...
○	... follow and give directions.
○	... plan a journey, book a hotel room and buy tickets.
○	... describe my physical condition.
○	... use ordinal numbers and talk about time and dates.
○	... talk about my health and refer to different parts of the body.

9

In this unit, you will learn how to:

» describe yourself and other people.
» use the simple past and present perfect tenses
» talk about what you have done.
» greet people during Norwegian holidays and festivities.

Snakk om fortiden

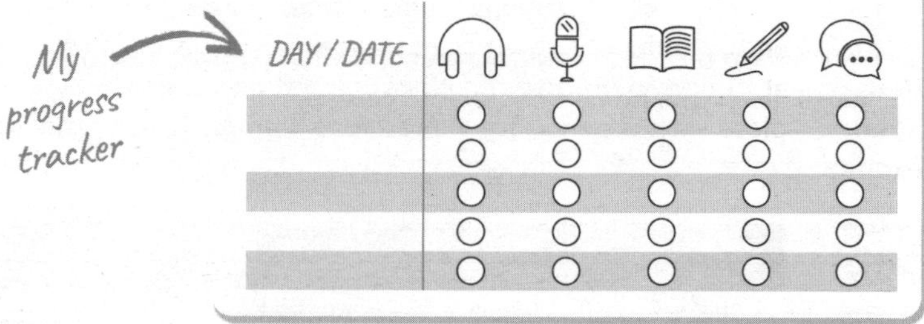

Norwegian holidays and festivities

Perhaps the most important holiday in Norway is **17. mai** (*17th May*), the day when Norwegians celebrate their **grunnlov** (*constitution*), signed in Eidsvoll on this day in 1814. People wear the **bunad** (*traditional folk costume*), carry the Norwegian **flagg** (*flag*) and greet each other saying **gratulerer med dagen** (*happy birthday*) and **hurra** (*cheer*), and singing **nasjonalsangen 'ja vi elsker'** (*the national anthem 'ja vi elsker'*). In terms of religious festivities, Norwegians celebrate **Luciadagen** (*St Lucy*) on 13th of December and bake a typical Swedish dish called **lussekatter** (*saffron buns*). **Jul** (*Christmas*) is very important in Norway, and it is very nice to see candles and Christmas lights everywhere. People greet each other saying **god jul** (*Merry Christmas*), exchange presents and eat traditional Christmas food, such as **lutefisk** (*lye fish*), **ribbe** (*pork roast*) or **pinnekjøtt** (*lamb or mutton roast*), depending on the region. Norwegians often discuss which of these dishes is the best Christmas dish, but in the end, it all comes down to **familjetradisjon** (*family tradition*). In Norway presents are exchanged on **julaften** (*24th December*), instead of on **1. juledag** (*25th December*), and *Boxing Day* is called **andre juledag**.

Nyttårsaften (*New Year's Eve*) is celebrated with **fyrverkeri** (*fireworks*) and by saying **godt nytt år / godt nyttår** (*Happy New Year*), as one also does on **nyttårsdag** (*New Year's Day*). Another very important religious holiday is **påske** (*Easter*), during which Norwegians eat lots of **egg** (*eggs*), take long trips to their **hytter** (*cabins*), **går på ski** (*go skiing*), and read **påskekrim** (*the Easter mystery novel*). Another non-religious festivity is **1. mai** (*the 1st of May*), also called **arbeidernes dag** (*Workers' Day*).

How do you think you would say *Happy Easter*?

Vocabulary builder

09.01 **Listen to the following verbs in the different tenses, and then repeat, trying to imitate the Norwegian pronunciation. Then complete with the missing expressions in English, as in the examples.**

Infinitive	Present	Simple past	Present perfect	English infinitive
å bøye	**bøyer**	**bøyde**	**har bøyd**	*to bend*
å drikke	**drikker**	**drakk**	**har drukket**	*to drink*
å feire	**feirer**	**feiret**	**har feiret**	*to celebrate*
å forstå	**forstår**	**forsto**	**har forstått**	*to understand*
å gjøre	**gjør**	**gjorde**	**har gjort**	
å glemme	**glemmer**	**glemte**	**har glemt**	
å gå	**går**	**gikk**	**har gått**	
å ha	**har**	**hadde**	**har hatt**	
å hate	**hater**	**hatet**	**har hatet**	
å høre	**hører**	**hørte**	**har hørt**	
å jobbe	**jobber**	**jobbet**	**har jobbet**	
å lage	**lager**	**lagde**	**har lagd**	
å leie	**leier**	**leide**	**har leid**	
å lese	**leser**	**leste**	**har lest**	
å nå	**når**	**nådde**	**har nådd**	
å se	**ser**	**så**	**har sett**	
å si	**sier**	**sa**	**har sagt**	
å skjønne	**skjønner**	**skjønte**	**har skjønt**	
å snakke	**snakker**	**snakket**	**har snakket**	
å spille	**spiller**	**spilte**	**har spilt**	
å spise	**spiser**	**spiste**	**har spist**	
å sy	**syr**	**sydde**	**har sydd**	
å tro	**tror**	**trodde**	**har trodd**	
å vente	**venter**	**ventet**	**har ventet**	
å være	**er**	**var**	**har vært**	*to be*

NEW EXPRESSIONS

Some of these new expressions are used in the following dialogues. Note their meaning and the differences between the various alternatives.

Jeg er 1,60 meter høy.	*I am 1.6 meters (5'3") tall.*
Jeg er flink (i noe).	*I am good (at something).*
Han er frekk.	*He is rude.*
Han er hyggelig.	*He is nice.*
Han er morsom.	*He is funny.*
Jeg er slem.	*I am naughty / bad.*
De er sta.	*They are stubborn.*
Hun er stolt.	*She is proud.*
Hun er sterk.	*She is strong.*
Du er svak.	*You are weak.*
Jeg har blå øyne.	*I have blue eyes.*
Jeg har brune øyne.	*I have brown eyes.*
Jeg har grønne øyne.	*I have green eyes.*
Jeg har blondt hår.	*I have blond hair.*
Jeg har rødt hår.	*I have red hair.*
Jeg har brunt hår.	*I have brown hair.*
Jeg har mørkt hår.	*I have dark hair.*
Jeg har lyst hår.	*I have fair hair.*

Dialogue 1

09.02 *It is the evening of* ***17. mai****, and Monika and Guri are talking about what they did and where they went during the day. Listen carefully to the dialogue before answering the questions.*

1 **What was Monika wearing?**

2 **Why was Guri dressed differently?**

Monika	Gratulerer med dagen!
Guri	Ja, gratulerer med dagen! Hvordan feiret du?
Monika	Jeg spiste 17. mai frokost hos noen venner, og så gikk jeg til Karl Johans gate tidlig for å se på barnetoget. Niesen min gikk sitt første tog i år!
Guri	Å, så koselig! Tok du mange bilder?
Monika	Ja, hun var veldig stolt av bunaden sin.
Guri	Jeg kan tenke meg det! Hadde du også bunad på?

Monika	Ja, hadde ikke du bunad på deg?
Guri	Nei, den ble igjen hos foreldrene mine i Nord-Norge, så jeg måtte ha en vanlig kjole på meg.
Monika	Jeg skjønner, neste år da.
Guri	Ja. Hva gjorde du etter toget?
Monika	Jeg og niesen spiste softis, mens søsteren min og mannen hennes spiste pølse, og så gikk vi til Grønland, for der er det Tivoli.
Guri	Jeg var også der! Synd at vi ikke så hverandre.
Monika	Ja, men det var fullt av folk.
Guri	Ja, det var nok det.

3 Re-read the dialogue and answer the following questions.

- **a** Where did Monika eat breakfast?
- **b** Where did she go after breakfast?
- **c** What did she do after the parade?
- **d** What did Monika eat?
- **e** What did her sister eat?
- **f** Where did both Monika and Guri go after the parade?

4 Look at the dialogue again, then match the Norwegian with the English translation.

- **a** Gratulerer med dagen!
- **b** Tok du mange bilder?
- **c** Hadde du også bunad på?
- **d** Jeg og niesa spiste softis, mens søstera mi og mannen hennes spiste pølse
- **e** Synd at vi ikke så hverandre.
- **f** Ja, men det var fullt av folk.

1. Yes, but it was crowded.
2. It's a pity we didn't see each other.
3. My niece and I ate soft-serve ice cream, while my sister and her husband ate a hot dog.
4. Did you take many pictures?
5. Happy birthday! / Happy 17th May!
6. Did you wear a *bunad* as well?

5 How do Guri and Monika say the following?

a parade

1 folk **2** pølse **3** softis **4** tog

b dress

1 folk **2** kjole **3** pølse **4** softis

c pictures
1 bilder   2 mange   3 softis   4 tog

d many
1 kjole   2 mange   3 pølse   4 softis

e people
1 bilder   2 folk   3 kjole   4 tog

f hot dog
1 kjole   2 mange   3 pølse   4 softis

g soft serve (ice cream)
1 kjole   2 mange   3 pølse   4 softis

Language discovery 1

SIMPLE PAST

In Norwegian, the simple past is created by changing the verb ending. Endings depend on which group the verb belongs to. There are four groups of regular verbs and then there are irregular verbs, which behave differently. It is useful to note that the irregular verbs often behave similarly to their English equivalents.

Irregular verbs

Jeg *drakk* te i går.	*I drank tea yesterday.*
Jeg *forsto* ikke.	*I didn't understand.*
Hun *gjorde* ikke det jeg *sa*.	*She didn't do what I said.*
***Var* du hjemme i går?**	*Were you at home yesterday?*

To make the simple past of regular verbs, we take out both the **å** and the **-e** ending of the infinitive, then add the tense ending, which changes according to which 'group' the verb belongs to.

Group 1

The ending for this group is **-et** (which in many dialects becomes **-a**). The majority of Norwegian verbs belong to this group: if the base form ends in **-d**, **-t**, or two consonants (e.g. **-nt**, **-sk**, etc.), then the verb belongs to this group.

1 Complete the following verbs with the definite ending.

a Jeg snakk_______ med Pål for tre dager siden.
I talked to Pål three days ago.

b Hun hat_______ ham etter bruddet.
She hated him after the break-up.

c Han vent_______ på henne på kafeen.
He waited for her at the coffee shop.

Group 2

The ending for this group is **-te**. If the base form ends in **-es**, **-ek**, **-is**, **-it**, **-øk**, **-ør**, **-ill**, **-emm,** etc., then the verb belongs to this group.

2 Complete the following verbs with the definite ending.

a Jeg les_______ hele dagen i går.
I studied / read all day yesterday.

b Han hør_______ alltid på musikk.
He always listened to music.

c Hun spil_______ fotball i går.
She played football yesterday.

d Han glem_______ nøklene hjemme i morges.
He forgot the keys at home this morning.

Group 3

The ending for this group is **-de**. If the base form ends in **-g**, **-v**, or in **-ei**, **-ai**, **-øy**, then the verb belongs to this group.

3 Complete the following verbs with the definite ending.

a Jeg lag_______ ei kake til hennes bursdag.
I made a cake for her birthday.

b Jeg lei_______ leiligheten min i fjor.
I rented my apartment last year.

c Læreren bøy_______ verbet for studentene.
The teacher conjugated the verb for the students.

Group 4

The ending for this group is **-dde**. If the verb has only one syllable, then it belongs to this group.

4 Complete the following verbs with the definite ending.

a Hun ha_______ mange venner. *She had many friends.*

b Jeg tro_______ ikke på ham. *I did not believe him.*

c Han nå_______ ikke flyplassen i tiden. *He did not reach the airport in time.*

d Hun sy_______ genseren min. *She sewed my sweater.*

Dialogue 2

09.03 *Olav and Ulf are talking about places they have been to, and places they would like to visit. Listen carefully to the dialogue before answering the questions.*

1 **Where has Olav never been?**

2 **Where would Ulf like to go next?**

Olav	Har du vært i Australia?
Ulf	Nei, jeg har aldri vært der, men neste gang jeg reiser, skal jeg dra til Australia og New Zealand, jeg har allerede bestilt flybillettene.
Olav	Så bra! Jeg har vært der én gang da jeg var ung, det var fantastisk!
Ulf	Ja, jeg gleder meg. Har du vært i Canada?
Olav	Ja, jeg har vært både i Canada og i USA, men det er lenge siden, jeg vil gjerne dra tilbake.
Ulf	Du har vært overalt!
Olav	Nei, jeg har aldri vært i Tyskland, så jeg tror jeg reiser dit neste gang.
Ulf	Jeg har vært i Tyskland mange ganger, men jeg har aldri vært i Østerrike. Jeg vil gjerne reise dit også. Har du vært der?
Olav	Ja, det har jeg, og jeg har også vært i Frankrike, Italia og Spania.
Ulf	Jeg har vært i Spania, men ikke i Frankrike og Italia.
Olav	Vi har aldri reist sammen, vi kunne gjøre det!
Ulf	Ja, det er en god idé, vi må bare finne et sted ingen av oss har sett før.
Olav	Det er sikkert lett, det er mange steder vi aldri har sett!
Ulf	Ja, det er sant.

3 **Re-read the dialogue and answer the following questions.**

a How many countries has Olav visited?
b Which are they?
c How many countries has Ulf visited?
d Which are they?
e What do they decide in the end?

4 Look at the conversation again, then match the Norwegian with the English translation.

a Jeg har vært der én gang da jeg var ung, det var fantastisk!

b Du har vært overalt!

c Vi har aldri reist sammen.

d Vi må bare finne et sted ingen av oss har sett før.

e Det er mange steder vi aldri har sett.

1 We have never traveled together.

2 We just have to find a place neither of us has seen before.

3 I have been there once when I was young, it was fantastic!

4 There are many places we have never seen.

5 You have been everywhere!

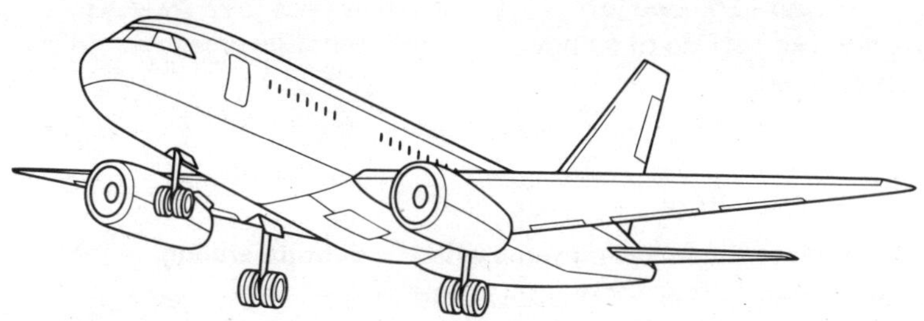

5 How do Olav and Ulf say the following?

a everywhere
- **1** både ... og
- **2** overalt
- **3** det er lenge siden
- **4** aldri

b both ... and
- **1** både ... og
- **2** overalt
- **3** det er lenge siden
- **4** ingen av oss

c it's been a long time
- **1** både ... og
- **2** overalt
- **3** det er lenge siden
- **4** ingen av oss

d neither of us
- **1** både ... og
- **2** det er lenge siden
- **3** aldri
- **4** ingen av oss

e never
- **1** både ... og
- **2** det er lenge siden
- **3** aldri
- **4** ingen av oss

Language discovery 2

PRESENT PERFECT

The present perfect in Norwegian is composed, as in English, of the verb *to have* in the present tense and the **past participle** of the verb.

Irregular verbs

Jeg *har* nettopp *drukket* te.	*I have just drunk tea.*
Jeg *har* ikke *forstått*.	*I haven't understood.*
Hun *har* ikke *gjort* det jeg sa.	*She hasn't done what I said.*
***Har* du *vært* hjemme hele dagen?**	*Have you been home all day?*
***Har* de *vært* i England før?**	*Have they been to England before?*
De har ikke hatt tid til å ringe meg ennå.	*They haven't had time to call me yet.*

Group 1

The ending for this group remains **-et**.

1 Complete the following verbs with the definite ending.

a Jeg har nettopp snakk________ med Pål.
I just talked to Pål.

b Hun har ikke jobb________ i dag.
She has not been working today.

c De har vent________ på oss i en time.
They have been waiting for us for one hour.

Group 2

The ending for this group is **-t**.

2 Complete the following verbs with the definite ending.

a Jeg har les________ hele dagen.
I have been studying / reading all day.

b Han har alltid hør________ på musikk.
He has always listened to music.

c Hun har spil________ fotball i to timer.
She has been playing football for two hours.

d Han har glem_______ nøklene hjemme.
He has forgotten the keys at home.

Group 3

The ending for this group is **-d**.

3 Complete the following verbs with the definite ending.

a Jeg har lag_______ ei kake.
I have made a cake.

b Jeg har lei_______ leiligheten min.
I have rented my apartment.

c Læreren har bøy_______ verbet.
The teacher has conjugated the verb.

Group 4

The ending for this group is **-dd**.

4 Complete the following verbs with the definite ending. Pay special attention to the verb *to have*.

a Hun har sy_______ genseren min.
She has sewn my sweater.

b Jeg har aldri tro_______ på ham.
I have never believed him.

c Han har ikke nå_______ flyplassen i tiden.
He has not reached the airport in time.

d Hun har ha_______ mange venner.
She has had many friends.

Practice

Rune and his partner are going to meet a distant relative, whom they have never met before, at the airport. Read the following email in which Rune describes himself and Åshild.

New message

Hei,

Jeg og Åshild vil vente på deg foran utgangen av internasjonale fly. Jeg er 1,80 meter høy, har rødt hår og blå øyne. Åshild er 1,70 meter høy, hun har grønne øyne og blondt hår.

Jeg kommer til å ha en rød genser på meg, og vi skal ta med babyen vår, hun er veldig liten og barnevogna hennes er lyseblå.

Vi ser frem til å treffe deg.

Med vennlig hilsen

Rune

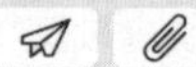

1 Re-read the email and answer the following questions.

- **a** How tall is Rune?
- **b** What color is Åshild's hair?
- **c** What color is Rune going to wear?
- **d** Who are they also bringing?
- **e** What color is her stroller?

2 How does Rune say the following?

- **a** 1.80 m tall
- **b** blond
- **c** red hair
- **d** blue eyes
- **e** We're looking forward to meeting you.

Test yourself

1 Talk about what you did when you were a child.

2 Rearrange the words into sentences; don't forget to place the capital letter on the first word.

a	vi	treffe	ser	til	frem	deg	å	.
b	ditt	for	som	deg	fyller	hurra	år	.
c	toget	du	hva	etter	gjorde	?		
d	folk	var	ja,	fullt	det	men	av	.
e	Australia	reiser	gang	jeg	neste	og	New	
	Zealand	til	.					
f	Spania vært	jeg	i	har	.			

3 Irregular verbs. Fill in the blanks with the simple past of the verb in brackets.

a Jeg ________ te i går. (*drink*)

b Jeg ________ ikke. (*understand*)

c Hun ________ ikke det jeg ________. (*do, say*)

d ________ du hjemme i går? (*be*)

4 Irregular verbs. Fill in the blanks with the present perfect of the verb in brackets.

a Jeg ________ nettopp ________ te. (*drink*)

b Jeg ________ ikke ________. (*understand*)

c Hun ________ ikke ________ det. (*do*)

d ________ du ________ hjemme i hele dagen? (*stay / be*)

e ________ de ________ i England før? (*be*)

5 Write a short story using the simple past and present perfect.

____

____

____

____

____

SELF CHECK

	I CAN ...
○	... describe myself and other people.
○	... use the simple past and present perfect tenses.
○	... talk about what I have done.
○	... greet people during Norwegian holidays and festivities.

10

In this unit, you will learn how to:

- » describe the weather.
- » use time expressions to say when something happened.
- » use comparatives and superlatives.
- » talk about hobbies and free-time activities.
- » talk about sport, music, books and what you like and dislike.

Hva gjør du når du har fri?

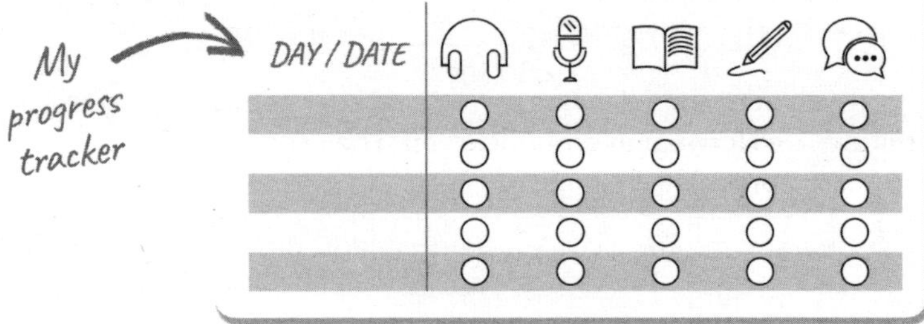

Geography, nature and climate

Norge (*Norway*) is one of the Scandinavian countries, together with **Sverige** (*Sweden*) and **Danmark** (*Denmark*), and it **grenser** (*adjoins*) **Sverige** (*Sweden*), **Finland** and **Russland** (*Russia*). Norway's **hovedstad** (*capital city*) is Oslo, and the country is divided into 15 **fylker** (*counties*). Norway is a **konstitusjonelt monarki** (*constitutional monarchy*), and its official name is **Kongeriket Norge**. Norway has around 5.5 million **innbyggere** (*inhabitants*), and is one of the world's **rikeste land** (*richest countries*). Norway is **langt** (*long*) and **smalt** (*narrow*), and it has a very long **kystlinje** (*coastline*), full of **fjorder** (*fjords*). The country also has many **fjell** (*mountains*), **skoger** (*forests*), **elver** (*rivers*) and **innsjøer** (*lakes*). Norway's **høyeste fjell** (*highest mountain*) is Galdhøpiggen, Norway's **største innsjø** (*largest lake*) is Mjøsa, and its **lengste elv** (*longest river*) is called Glomma. **Golfstrømmen** (*the Gulf Stream*) influences **klimaet** (*the climate*); **årsmiddeltemperaturen** (*the average yearly temperature*) is 8° C on the west coast, and 0° C in central mountain areas 750–1,000 **meter over havet** (*meters above sea level*). Norway's natural landscape changes greatly depending on the area. In **Nord-Norge** (one of the counties, called *North-Norway*) and on the mountains in the south, there is **arktiske plantearter** (*arctic plant life*), while on the coast in **Vestlandet** (one of the major areas into which Norway is divided), the plants are similar to those found in England, owing to the mitigating effect of the Gulf Stream. Typical animals in the north of Norway are **rein** (*reindeer*), the **jerv** (*wolverine*), **snøugle** (*snowy owl*), **ryper** (*lagopus*) and **snøspurv** (*snow bunting*). In the south of Norway one can find the **elg** (*moose*), **hjort** (*red deer*), **rådyr** (*roe deer*), **bever** (*European beaver*), **brunbjørn** (*brown bear*), **ulv** (*wolf*), **gaupe** (*Eurasian lynx*), **rev** (*fox*), **lemen** (*Norway lemming*) and **røyskatt** (*stoat*). On the whole coastline, there are also **hvaler** and **seler**.

a What are hvaler? **b What are seler?**

Vocabulary builder

10.01 Listen to the following words, and then repeat, trying to imitate the Norwegian pronunciation. Then complete with the missing expressions in English.

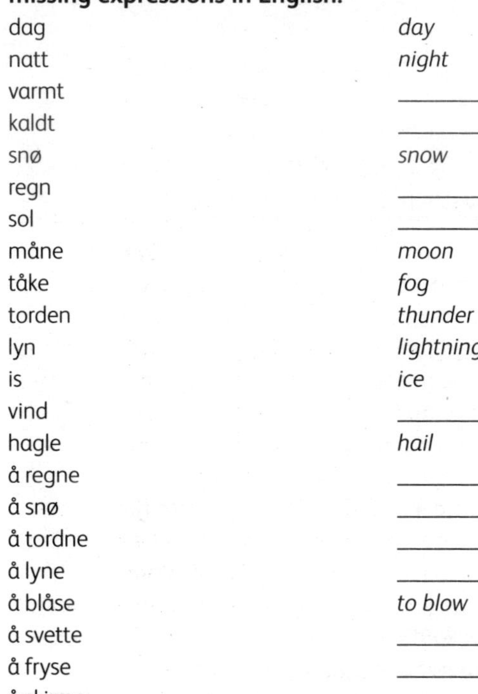

dag	*day*
natt	*night*
varmt	______
kaldt	______
snø	*snow*
regn	______
sol	______
måne	*moon*
tåke	*fog*
torden	*thunder*
lyn	*lightning*
is	*ice*
vind	______
hagle	*hail*
å regne	______
å snø	______
å tordne	______
å lyne	______
å blåse	*to blow*
å svette	______
å fryse	______
å skinne	______

NEW EXPRESSIONS

Some of these new expressions are used in the following dialogues. Note their meaning and the differences between the various alternatives.

Sola skinner.	*The sun is shining.*
Det er varmt.	*It's warm.*
Det er kaldt.	*It's cold.*
Været er fint.	*The weather is nice.*
Det er pent vær (i dag).	*The weather is nice (today).*
Det er dårlig vær (i dag).	*The weather is bad (today).*
Det er tåke.	*It's foggy.*
Det regner. / Det er regn.	*It's raining.*
Det tordner og lyner.	*There's thunder and lightning.*
Det snør.	*It's snowing.*
Det blåser. / Det er vind.	*It's windy.*
Det er is.	*There's ice.*
Det hagler.	*It's hailing.*
Jeg fryser.	*I'm freezing.*
Jeg er kald.	*I'm cold.*
Jeg er varm.	*I'm warm.*
Jeg svetter.	*I'm sweating.*
Det er 15° kuldegrader.	*It's 15 degrees (centigrade) below zero.*
Det er 30° (varme)grader.	*It's 30 degrees (centigrade).*

1 Match the Norwegian with its English translation.

a snø	**1** moon
b lyn	**2** thunder
c hagle	**3** lightning
d måne	**4** snow
e torden	**5** hail

Dialogue 1

10.02 *It's winter and it is very cold outside. Marit and Kristian talk about their favorite seasons, weather conditions and what they usually do during the different seasons. Listen carefully to the dialogue before answering the questions.*

1 What is Marit's favorite winter activity?

2 What does Kristian usually do during the winter?

Marit	Å, jeg fryser, det er så kaldt!
Kristian	Ja, du har rett, men jeg liker når det er vinter og det snør.
Marit	Ja da, jeg liker også snøen og det er koselig å være hjemme om vinteren, men jeg liker ikke at det er mørkt.
Kristian	Hva gjør du vanligvis om vinteren?
Marit	Om vinteren går jeg på ski, men jeg liker best å gå på skøyter. Og så drar jeg på hyttetur, selvfølgelig! Hva med deg?
Kristian	Jeg går mye på ski, men jeg går også tur i skogen når det er snø. Hvilken årstid liker du best?
Marit	Jeg liker våren best, været blir pent og det er blomster overalt. Hva med deg?
Kristian	Jeg liker sommeren veldig godt.
Marit	Hva gjør du vanligvis om sommeren?
Kristian	Jeg reiser ofte til Syden og nyter solen på stranden.
Marit	Å, det er nydelig! Jeg reiser også, men liker best å reise til varme steder om vinteren.
Kristian	Jeg skjønner. Det er også smart.
Marit	Ja, det er fint å ta en pause fra is og snø.

3 Re-read the dialogue and answer the following questions.

a Is Marit cold?
b What is Marit's favorite season?
c What does Kristian usually do during the summer?
d Where do they like traveling?

4 Look at the dialogue again, then match the Norwegian with the English translation.

a Du har rett.
b Jeg liker også snøen.
c Om vinteren går jeg på ski.
d Jeg liker best å gå på skøyter.
e Jeg liker våren best.
f Hva gjør du vanligvis om sommeren?

1 I ski during the winter.
2 You're right.
3 I prefer spring.
4 What do you normally do in the summer?
5 I like snow too.
6 I prefer skating.

5 How do Kristian and Marit say the following?

a usually / normally
  1 mørk
  2 vanligvis
  3 hyttetur
  4 selvfølgelig
  5 ofte

b dark
  1 mørk
  2 vanligvis
  3 hyttetur
  4 selvfølgelig
  5 ofte

c surely
  1 mørk
  2 vanligvis
  3 hyttetur
  4 selvfølgelig
  5 ofte

d often
  1 mørk
  2 vanligvis
  3 hyttetur
  4 selvfølgelig
  5 ofte

e trip to the cabin
  1 mørk
  2 vanligvis
  3 hyttetur
  4 selvfølgelig
  5 ofte

f season
  1 vinter
  2 årstid
  3 vår
  4 sommer
  5 høst

g winter
  1 vinter
  2 årstid
  3 vår
  4 sommer
  5 høst

h spring
  1 vinter
  2 årstid
  3 vår
  4 sommer
  5 høst

i summer
  1 vinter
  2 årstid
  3 vår
  4 sommer
  5 høst

j autumn / fall
  1 vinter
  2 årstid
  3 vår
  4 sommer
  5 høst

6 Rearrange the words into sentences, not forgetting to place the capital letter on the first word. Each sentence can be rearranged in two different ways. Write both.

a koselig er å vinteren være det hjemme om .

b ski vinteren om jeg på går .

c best vinteren liker å steder varme reise om til jeg .

d jeg lange går turer i om skogen sommeren .

e	pent	våren	blir	og	overalt	om	det	været
	er	blomster	.					
f	Syden	høsten	ofte	til	og	nyter	jeg	på
	sola	reiser	om	stranda	.			

Language discovery 1

TIME EXPRESSIONS

In Norwegian there are several ways to express when it is that something happens. Depending on when we are talking about, we must also use the right tense. Note that only the simple past is used with time expressions like those in the following table, and in these cases, they are used to express a finished action.

Past		Present		Future	
i morges	*this morning*	**nå**	*now*	**i morgen**	*tomorrow*
i går	*yesterday*	**i dag**	*today*	**(i) neste uke**	*next week*
i forrige uke	*last week*	**(i) denne uka**	*this week*	**om to / tre / fire ... dager / uker / måneder / år**	*in two / three / four days / weeks / months / years*
(i) forrige måned	*last month*	**i kveld**	*this evening*	**i morgen tidlig / ettermiddag / kveld**	*tomorrow morning / afternoon / evening*
i fjor	*last year*	**i år**	*this year*	**neste mandag / torsdag ...**	*next Monday / Tuesday ...*
for to / tre / fire ... år/ måneder / dager siden	*two / three / four ... years / months / days ago*	**i natt**	*tonight*	**neste uke / måned / år**	*next week / month / year*

We can also use time expressions with the present perfect tense, but only when we are talking about an action that is not over yet, or about something that just happened. Look at these examples.

Jeg har *akkurat* kommet hit.	*I have just arrived here.*
Hun har *nettopp* dratt.	*She has just gone away.*
Jeg har lest *i hele dagen*.	*I have been reading all day.*
Han har vært på ferie *i en måned*.	*He has been on holiday for one month.*

1 Match the Norwegian with the English translations.

a Hun kom til Australia for ei uke siden.
b Hanne har jobbet i fire timer.
c Dere har vært gift i seksti år.
d Dere var gift i seksti år.
e Hanne jobbet i fire timer.
f Han har vært syk i tre måneder.
g Hun flyttet til Spania i fjor.
h Han var syk i tre måneder.

1 She came to Australia a week ago.
2 You were married for 60 years.
3 She moved to Spain last year.
4 He has been ill for three months.
5 Hanne has been working for four hours.
6 You have been married for 60 years.
7 Hanne worked for four hours.
8 He was ill for three months.

2 Choose the correct meaning of the following expressions.

a dag
  1 yesterday
  2 today
  3 day

b natt
  1 today
  2 night
  3 day

c i dag
  1 yesterday
  2 today
  3 day

d i går
  1 tomorrow
  2 yesterday
  3 today

e i morgen
  1 tomorrow
  2 yesterday
  3 this morning

f i morges
  1 tomorrow
  2 yesterday
  3 this morning

g i fjor
  1 yesterday
  2 next year
  3 last year

h neste år
  1 tomorrow
  2 next year
  3 last year

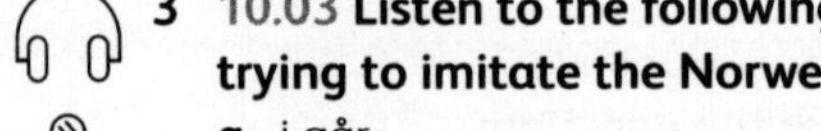

3 10.03 Listen to the following words, translate and repeat them, trying to imitate the Norwegian pronunciation.

a i går
b en dag
c i morges
d i fjor
e i oktober
f i dag
g i sommer
h i morgen
i om sommeren
j neste år
k om vinteren
l i julen
m i påsken
n en årstid

Dialogue 2

10.04 *Jorun and Yngve are talking about their favorite pastimes. Listen carefully to the dialogue before answering the questions.*

1 What are Jorun's favorite pastimes?

2 What are Yngve's favorite pastimes?

Jorun	Hva liker du å gjøre når du har fri?
Yngve	Jeg liker å lese, å høre på musikk, og å gå tur. Hva med deg?
Jorun	Jeg liker også å lese, å høre på musikk og å gå tur, men jeg liker også å spille brettspill med venner og å spille dataspill.
Yngve	Jeg også, jeg elsker å spille! Vi kunne spille sammen noen ganger.
Jorun	Ja, det er en kjempegod idé. Jeg bare ønsker vi hadde mer fritid.
Yngve	Ja, det er sant. Hva leser du vanligvis?
Jorun	Jeg liker krim og romaner, både på norsk og på engelsk. Og du?
Yngve	Nå leser jeg mange eventyr fra forskjellige land, jeg synes det er mer spennende å lese eldre enn nyere litteratur. Og man skjønner også flere moderne verk når man kjenner eldre litteratur.
Jorun	Ja, absolutt. Hvordan fikk du interesse for det?
Yngve	Jeg leste om sagn og mytologi, og så fikk jeg lyst til å lære mer om eventyr også, jeg har alltid vært interessert i nordisk litteratur og kultur.
Jorun	Det er veldig interessant, kanskje jeg skal også lese mer om det.

3 Read the dialogue again and answer the questions.

a What do they decide to do together?
b What is Yngve reading now?
c Why is he reading it?
d What does Jorun say at the end?

4 Look at the conversation again, then match the Norwegian with the English translation.

a Hva liker du å gjøre når du har fri?
b Jeg liker også å spille brettspill med venner.
c Ja, det er en kjempegod idé.
d Jeg bare ønsker vi hadde mer fritid.
e Jeg har alltid vært interessert i nordisk litteratur og kultur.

1 I have always been interested in Nordic literature and culture.
2 Yes, it's a great idea.
3 I like playing board games with friends too.
4 What do you like doing in your free time?
5 I only wish we had more free time.

5 How do Jorun and Yngve say the following?

a interesting
  1 kjempegod
  2 interessant
  3 vanligvis
  4 forskjellig

b usually
  1 kanskje
  2 vanligvis
  3 forskjellig
  4 absolutt

c maybe
  1 interessant
  2 kanskje
  3 vanligvis
  4 forskjellig

d different
  1 kjempegod
  2 vanligvis
  3 forskjellig
  4 absolutt

e absolutely
  1 kjempegod
  2 vanligvis
  3 forskjellig
  4 absolutt

f great / very good / wonderful
  1 kjempegod
  2 interessant
  3 vanligvis
  4 forskjellig

g more
  1 kjempegod
  2 interessant
  3 kanskje
  4 flere

Language discovery 2

1 COMPARATIVES AND SUPERLATIVES (INDEFINITE)

When we have to compare and contrast, we need to modify the adjectives. In Norwegian, the comparative is made by taking the base form of the adjective and adding the ending **-ere**, or **-re**, and often the word **enn**, as in the following example:

Denne genseren er *billigere enn* den der borte.	*This sweater is cheaper than the one over there.*

1 **Complete the following sentences with the correct comparative.**
   - **a** I dag er det kald_______ enn i går. *Today it is colder than yesterday.*
   - **b** Bilen min er ny_______ enn din. *My car is newer than yours.*

In some cases, the ending is not the only thing that changes in the base form.

2 **Complete the following sentences with the correct comparative.**
   - **a** Du er yng_______ enn meg. *You're younger than me.*
   - **b** Min søster er vakr_______ enn meg. *My sister is prettier than me.*
   - **c** Denne filmen er morsomm_______ enn den vi så i går. *This movie is funnier than the one we saw yesterday.*
   - **d** Det bordet er tungt, men dette er tyng_______. *That table is heavy, but this one is heavier.*

Norwegian superlatives are made by taking the base form of the adjective and adding the ending **-est**, or **-st**.

3 **Complete the following sentences with the correct superlative.**
   - **a** Denne genseren er billig_______. *This sweater is the cheapest.*
   - **b** Denne kjolen er dyr_______. *This dress is the most expensive.*
   - **c** Det er enkl_______ å ta buss. *It's easiest to take the bus.*
   - **d** Du er pen_______. *You're the prettiest.*

When the base form changes for the comparative, then it also changes for the superlative, adding the ending **-est**, or **-st**.

4 **Complete the following sentences with the correct superlative.**
   - **a** Jeg er yng_______. *I'm the youngest.*
   - **b** Du er vakr_______. *You're the prettiest.*
   - **c** Dette bordet er tyng_______. *This table is the heaviest.*

As in English, Norwegian has some irregular adjectives, which, instead of taking a different ending, need the word **mer** (*more*), and **mest** (*most*).

5 Complete the following sentences with the correct comparative or superlative.

- **a** Det er _______ praktisk å ta trikken. *It's more practical to take the tram.*
- **b** Å ta trikken er _______ praktisk. *To take the tram is most practical.*

Other irregular adjectives change completely from the base form to the comparative, and then maintain the changes in the superlative form as well, such as **bra–bedre–best** (*good–better–best*) and **mange–flere–flest** (*many–more–most*).

6 Complete the following sentences with the correct comparative or superlative.

a	Det går _______ .	*I'm good. / It's good.*
b	Det går _______ .	*I'm better. / It's better.*
c	Det er _______ at vi går hjem.	*It's best if we go home.*
d	Det er _______ folk.	*There are many people.*
e	Det er _______ folk.	*There are more people.*
f	Folk _______ er her.	*Most people are here.*

7 Match the Norwegian with the English.

a bedre	**1** a little
b dårlig / ille	**2** bad
c eldst	**3** better
d færre	**4** few
e færrest	**5** fewer
f få	**6** fewest
g gammel	**7** good / well
h god / bra	**8** less
i lite	**9** many
j mange	**10** more
k mer	**11** most
l mest	**12** much
m mindre	**13** old
n mye	**14** oldest
o verre	**15** worse

2 SUPERLATIVES (DEFINITE)

If the superlative comes after a demonstrative pronoun (**den**, **det**, **de**, etc.), it has an **-e** added at the end, as with the plural form:

Han er *den snilleste* jeg kjenner.	*He's the nicest I know.*
Du er *den morsomste* jeg kjenner.	*You're the funniest I know.*
Hanne kjøpte *det dyreste* huset.	*Hanne bought the most expensive house.*
Guro har *den peneste* kjolen.	*Guro has the prettiest dress.*

3 SIMPLE PAST AND PRESENT PERFECT OF MODAL VERBS

The simple past of modal verbs is the same as the infinitive form of the verb, but without the **å**.

***Kunne* han komme i går?**	*Could he come yesterday?*
Hva *ville* du si?	*What did you want to say?*
***Måtte* du vente lenge?**	*Did you have to wait for a long time?*

Sometimes, the simple past of modal verbs is used as a conditional, or to ask something politely, as in the following examples:

Vi *kunne* spise ute i kveld.	*We could eat out tonight.*
***Burde* du ikke lese?**	*Shouldn't you study?*

Present perfect of modal verbs is made by adding the present form of the verb *to have* (**har**), and the ending **-t** to the infinitive without the **å**:

Jeg *har måttet* dra hjem tidligere.	*I had to go home sooner.*
Jeg *har* ikke *kunnet* komme tidligere.	*I couldn't come sooner.*

Practice

1 10.05 Listen to Dialogue 1 again, fill in the blanks and read it out loud.

Marit	Å, jeg ________ , det er så ________ !
Kristian	Ja, du har rett, men jeg liker når det er ________ og det ________ .
Marit	Ja da, jeg liker også ________ og det er koselig å være hjemme om ________ , men jeg liker ikke at ________ .
Kristian	Hva gjør du vanligvis om ________ ?
Marit	________ vinteren går jeg på ski, men jeg liker best å gå på ________ . Og så drar jeg på ________ , selvfølgelig! Hva med deg?
Kristian	Jeg går mye på ski, men jeg går også tur i skogen når det er ________ . Hvilken ________ liker du best?
Marit	Jeg liker ________ best, været blir pent og det er ________ overalt. Hva med deg?
Kristian	Jeg liker ________ veldig godt.
Marit	Hva gjør du vanligvis ________ ?
Kristian	Jeg ________ ofte til Syden og nyter ________ på stranden.
Marit	Å, det er nydelig! Jeg reiser også, men liker best å reise til ________ steder om ________ .
Kristian	Jeg skjønner. Det er også ________ .
Marit	Ja, det er fint å ta ________ fra is og snø.

2 Åse is studying abroad for a year and she writes an email to her younger brother in Norway, telling him what she has been doing. Read her email and answer the questions.

New message

Fra: Åse
Til: Vebjørn
Dato: 16.01.2025
Objekt: Oppdatering om studentliv.

Hei lillebror,

Hvordan har du det? Jeg har det fint og trives veldig godt her, og jeg må absolutt fortelle deg hva jeg har gjort i det siste!

I går tok vi en klassetur til London, hvor vi så The British Museum og The National Gallery, men det jeg likte best var Madame Tussauds! Jeg har aldri sett noe liknende, du må komme og se det! Om kvelden var vi veldig trøtte, så det var flott at vi dro tilbake til Oxford med en privatbuss.

I de siste ukene har jeg også spilt mange forskjellige typer sport, vi spiller basketball hver mandag, og hver onsdag spiller vi volleyball, jeg har prøvd å spille cricket, men jeg er ikke flink. Vi har også prøvd å spille tennis, men jeg liker det ikke. På lørdag gikk jeg og min venninne Amber på svømmehallen og svømte i to timer, det er fortsatt min favorittsport!

Nå må jeg gå, for vi skal på teater for å se *A Midsummer Night's Dream*. Jeg gleder meg masse!

Klemmer

Åse

- **a** Where is Åse studying?
- **b** What did she do yesterday?
- **c** What was her favorite activity?
- **d** Which sports did she practice in the last few weeks?
- **e** Which one is her favorite?

3 How does Åse say the following?

a I like it here
b similar
c tired
d little brother
e swimming pool
f favorite
g hugs
h still
i a lot

CULTURE TIP

Idrett (*sport*) is very popular in Norway, which is a world leader in **vinteridretter** (*winter sports*), such as **langrenn** (*cross-country skiing*). Since the 1990s, Norway has also become better at **sommeridrettene** (*summer sports*), such as **400 m hekk** (*400m hurdles*).

If students want to become professional **idrettsutøvere** (*athletes*), they can choose **idrettsfag** (*sports studies*) in high school, so that they can **trene** (*practice*) and study at the same time.

Test yourself

1 Tell someone what you have been doing lately.

2 Rearrange the words into sentences; don't forget to place the capital letter on the first word.

a	er	dag	kaldt	det	veldig	i	.		
b	har	hun	dratt	nettopp	.				
c	ferie	i	har	måned	vært	han	på	en	.
d	år	tre	bodde	i	Norge	hun	siden	for	.
e	kom	hjem	du	når	,	ute	jeg		
	var	.							

3 Write a short text in which you talk about your favorite sports and activities you do at different times of the year.

___

___

___

___

SELF CHECK

	I CAN ...
○	... describe the weather.
○	... use time expressions to say when something happened.
○	... use comparatives and superlatives.
○	... talk about hobbies, sport and free-time activities
○	... talk about what I like and dislike

R3 Review 3

7 Vi skal ut og spise

1 Match the Norwegian with the English.

a	**klima**	**1**	milk
b	**bær**	**2**	vegetables
c	**frukt**	**3**	soft serve (ice cream)
d	**pannekake**	**4**	fishball
e	**skalldyr**	**5**	butter
f	**fisk**	**6**	pancake
g	**kosthold**	**7**	fruit
h	**grønnsaker**	**8**	fish
i	**fiskebolle**	**9**	climate
j	**kjøtt**	**10**	berries
k	**melk**	**11**	crustaceans
l	**softis**	**12**	meat
m	**smør**	**13**	diet

2 Translate the following sentences into English.

a Jeg synes det.
b Vil du ha noe å drikke?
c Er du klar til å bestille?
d Hva vil du drikke?
e Vil du ha noe annet?
f Dette barnet heter Hans.
g Smak til med salt og pepper.
h Jeg spiser ikke mat som kommer fra dyr, jeg er veganer.

3 Translate the following sentences into Norwegian and say them out loud.

a Does it taste good?
b What would you like?
c Do you want anything else?
d Would you like something to drink?

e Do you want to order?
f Cut the meat into cubes.
g Add potatoes.
h Serve with wholemeal bread.

4 Fill in the blanks with the verb in the imperative form.

a _______ hit! (komme)
b _______ engelsk! (snakke)
c _______ på norsk! (skrive)
d _______ smør. (tilsette)
e _______ hjem! (gå)
f _______ meg være i fred! (la)
g _______ mamma nå! (ringe)
h _______ kaka! (spise)

5 Complete the following crossword.

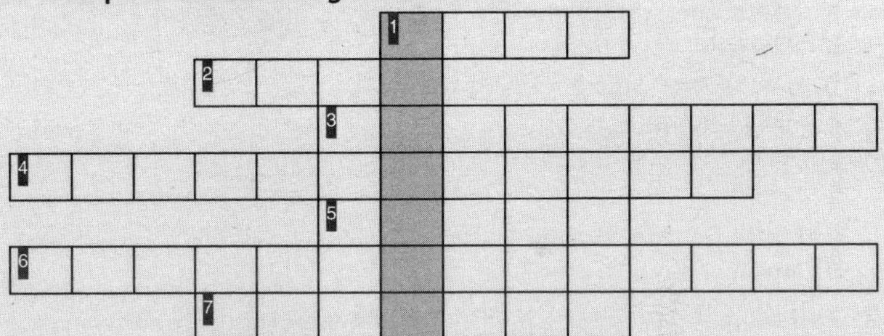

Across:

What is the Norwegian for the following?

1 bread
2 butter
3 carrots
4 hazelnuts
5 tomato
6 blueberry jam
7 garlic

Down:

Have you found the mystery word? What is it? _______

8 På ferie i Norge

1 Translate the following sentences into English.

a Hvor ligger museet?
b Hvor ligger sykehuset?
c Jeg har vondt i magen.
d Jeg har vondt i halsen.
e Gå rett fram.
f Jeg vil gjerne se julehuset!
g Jeg synes det passer bra.
h Hvor vil dere bo?
i Jeg fryser.

2 Translate the following sentences into Norwegian and say them out loud.

a Where is the souvenir shop?
b How much do the tickets cost?
c How long are you staying?
d Where can we eat?
e Please, can you help me?
f I am ill.
g I want to book the room online.
h I'm buying my train ticket on the app.

3 Write a postcard in which you describe your trip to Norway.

4 Complete the following crossword.

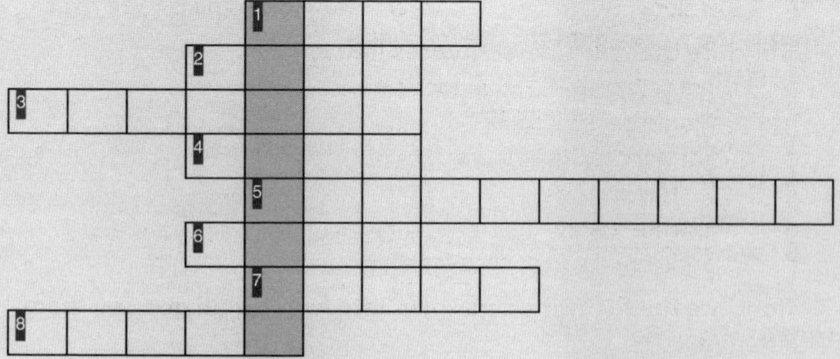

Across:

What is the Norwegian for the following?

1 throat
2 head
3 shoulder
4 nose
5 index (finger)
6 cheek
7 nape
8 elbow

Down:

Have you found the mystery word? What is it? ________

9 Snakk om fortiden

1 Match the Norwegian with the English.

a	Jeg er hyggelig.	**1**	I am proud.
b	Jeg har lyst hår.	**2**	I am nice.
c	Jeg har blondt hår.	**3**	I am strong.
d	Jeg er stolt.	**4**	I have light hair.
e	Jeg er sterk.	**5**	I have red hair.
f	Jeg har rødt hår.	**6**	I have blue eyes.
g	Jeg har blå øyne.	**7**	I have dark hair.
h	Jeg har mørk hår.	**8**	I am naughty / bad.
i	Jeg er slem.	**9**	I have blond hair.

2 Translate the following sentences into English.

a Hun var veldig stolt av bunaden sin.
b Hva gjorde du etter toget?
c Synd at vi ikke så hverandre.
d Det var fullt av folk.
e Han glemte nøklene hjemme i morges.
f Jeg lagde ei kake til hennes bursdag.

3 Translate the following sentences into Norwegian and say them out loud.

a I drank tea yesterday.
b Were you at home yesterday?
c I talked to Pål three days ago.
d He waited for her at the coffee shop.
e She had many friends.

- **f** He did not reach the airport in time.
- **g** She hasn't done what I said.
- **h** We have been waiting for them for one hour.
- **i** I have made a cake.
- **j** I have never believed him.

4 Fill in the blanks with the verb in the correct tense.

- **a** Jeg ________ aldri ________ på ham. (å tro)
- **b** Jeg ________ ikke. (å forstå)
- **c** Jeg ________ i hele dagen. (å lese)
- **d** Hun ________ ikke det jeg sa. (å gjøre)
- **e** Hun ________ mange venner. (å ha)
- **f** ________ du hjemme i går? (å være)
- **g** Hun ________ ham etter bruddet. (å hate)
- **h** Jeg ________ ei kake. (å lage)
- **i** Jeg ________ hele dagen i går. (å lese)
- **j** Hun ________ fotball i to timer. (å spille)
- **k** Han ________ alltid på musikk. (å høre)
- **l** Jeg ________ ikke på ham. (å tro)
- **m** Jeg ________ nettopp ________ te. (å drikke)
- **n** Hun ________ mange venner. (å ha)
- **o** Hun ________ på dem i en time. (å vente)

5 Complete the following crossword.

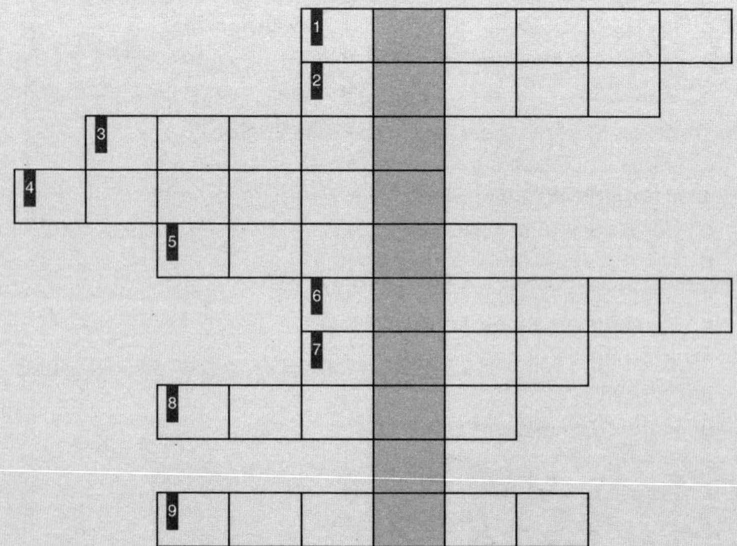

Across:

What is the simple past of the following verbs?

1 eat
2 drink
3 make
4 work
5 hate
6 believe
7 go
8 read
9 forget

Down:

Have you completed the mystery word? What is it? ________

10 Hva gjør du når du har fri?

1 Match the Norwegian with the English.

a	**hovedstad**	1	lake
b	**grense**	2	lynx
c	**elv**	3	wolf
d	**innsjø**	4	whale
e	**reinsdyr**	5	capital
f	**gaupe**	6	mountain
g	**ulv**	7	river
h	**hval**	8	forest
i	**fjell**	9	border
j	**skog**	10	reindeer

2 Translate the following sentences into English.

a Det er varmt.
b Været er fint.
c Det er dårlig vær.
d Det tordner og lyner.
e Det snør.
f Det hagler.
g Det er 15° kuldegrader.

3 Translate the following sentences into Norwegian and say them out loud.

a The sun is shining.
b It's cold.
c It's foggy.
d It's raining.
e It's windy.
f There's ice.
g I'm cold.
h I'm warm.
i I'm sweating.

4 Fill in the blanks with the correct word. Look at the words in brackets for help.

a Jeg bare ønsker vi hadde ________ fritid. (*more*)
b Nå leser jeg ________ eventyr fra ________ land. (*many, different*)
c Det er ________ . (*very interesting*)
d I dag er det ________ enn i går. (*colder*)
e Du er ________ enn meg. (*younger*)
f Denne kjolen er ________ . (*most expensive*)
g Du er ________ . (*most beautiful*)
h Å ta trikken er ________ . (*more practical*)
i Det går ________ . (*better*)
j Det er ________ folk. (*more*)
k Hanne kjøpte det ________ huset. (*most expensive*)
l Han er den ________ jeg kjenner. (*kindest*)
m Guro har den ________ kjolen. (*prettiest*)

5 Complete the following crossword.

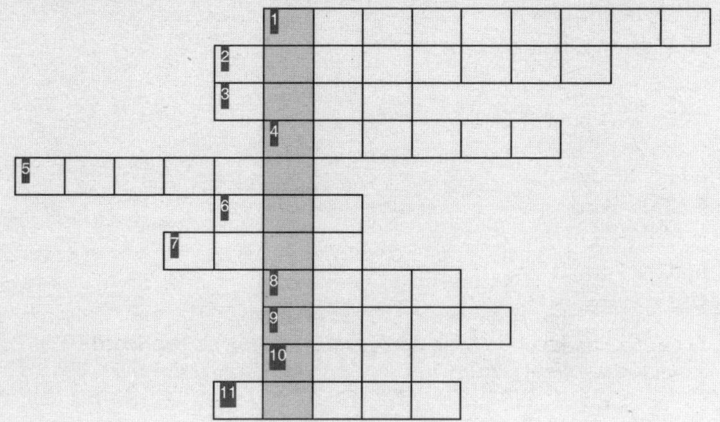

Across:

What is the Norwegian for the following?

1 exciting
2 boring
3 cold
4 untidy
5 funny
6 pretty
7 warm
8 original
9 Norwegian
10 expensive
11 fresh

Down:

Have you found the mystery word? What is it? ________

Answer key

UNIT 1

Discovery question: Thank you for the meal

Vocabulary builder

God dag!	*Good day! / Good morning!*
God morgen!	*Good morning!*
God kveld! / God aften!	*Good evening!*
Vi ses! / Vi sees!	*See you!*
God natt!	*Good night!*
Takk for maten!	*Thanks for the food!*

Dialogue 1

1 At the university
2 No
3 a. 2/4; **b.** 3; **c.** 4/2; **d.** 1
4 He comes from Tromsø.
5 She comes from Lillehammer.
6 a. 2; **b.** 1; **c.** 1; **d.** 2
7 a. heter; **b.** kommer
8 a. du; **b.** hun

Language discovery 1

1 a. 6; **b.** 1; **c.** 5; **d.** 2; **e.** 3; **f.** 7; **g.** 4
2 a. meg; **b.** henne
3 Hun heter Maja, hun er norsk, hun bor i Norge og hun jobber i Oslo. Hun har en hund og en katt. Hun går ut, treffer venner og snakker med dem. Hun liker Norge.

Dialogue 2

1 No
2 London
3 a. They are friends; **b.** She is waiting for the tram; **c.** She is a teacher; **d.** She lives in Oslo
4 a. 2; **b.** 1; **c.** 4; **d.** 3

5 a. Jeg er ferdig på jobb og venter på trikken; **b.** Jeg kommer fra London, men jeg bor i Oslo; **c.** Trikken kommer
6 a. 1; **b.** 3
7 very, really
8 good (at something)

Language discovery 2
2 a. 7; **b.** 2; **c.** 4; **d.** 5; **e.** 1; **f.** 3; **g.** 6

Practice
1

Maja	Abby? So nice to see you again! What are you doing here?
Abby	Hi! Long time no see! I have finished work and I'm waiting for the tram.
Maja	Erlend, this is my friend Abby Becker; she's a teacher.
Erlend	Nice meeting you, Abby.
Abby	Likewise.
Erlend	Where are you from?
Abby	I'm from London, but I live in Oslo.
Erlend	Your Norwegian is very good!
Abby	Thanks! The tram is coming, see you soon. Bye!

2 a. They are friends; **b.** He is an old friend; **c.** He is a biologist at the University of Oslo; **d.** Ella is from Trondheim; **e.** She is an actress; **f.** She works at the University of Oslo, she is a chemist and she does research.
3 også

Test yourself
1 a. Hun snakker med ham; **b.** Hvordan har du det?; **c.** Kommer du fra Frankrike?; **d.** Jeg er biolog og bor i Norge. / Jeg bor i Norge og er biolog; **e.** Hva heter dere?
2 a. Hyggelig å treffe / møte deg; **b.** Takk for sist; **c.** Ha det (bra); **d.** God morgen
3 a. Hvordan har du det?; **b.** Hva heter du?; **c.** Hvor kommer du fra?; **d.** Hvordan går det?
4 a. 3; **b.** 4; **c.** 5; **d.** 2; **e.** 6; **f.** 1

UNIT 2

Discovery question: -isk and -sk

Vocabulary builder

Languages

svensk	*Swedish*
spansk	*Spanish*
skotsk	*Scottish*
samisk	*Sami*
russisk	*Russian*
portugisisk	*Portuguese*
polsk	*Polish*
norsk	*Norwegian*
nederlandsk	*Dutch*
italiensk	*Italian*
islandsk	*Icelandic*
irsk	*Irish*
hindi	*Hindi*
fransk	*French*
finsk	*Finnish*
færøysk	*Faroese*
engelsk	*English*
dansk	*Danish*
arabisk	*Arabic*

Nationalities

amerikaner	*American*
danske	*Dane*
engelskmann	*Englishman / Englishwoman*
finne	*Finn*
franskmann	*Frenchman / Frenchwoman*
inder	*Indian*
ire	*Irishman / Irishwoman*
islending	*Icelander*
italiener	*Italian*
nederlender	*Dutchman / Dutchwoman*
nordmann	*Norwegian*
polakk	*Pole*
portugiser	*Portuguese*

russer	*Russian*
skotte	*Scot*
spanjol	*Spaniard*
sveitser	*Swiss*
svenske	*Swede*
østerriker	*Austrian*

New expressions

1 hvilken / hvilket / hvilke

2a. masculine / feminine **b.** neuter **c.** masculine / feminine **d.** plural

Dialogue 1

1 Norwegian, French, English and German

2 Italian

3 a. Hindi; **b.** To find out if it is difficult; **c.** Portuguese

4 a. 2; **b.** 4; **c.** 1; **d.** 3

5 a. 2; **b.** 3; **c.** 2

6 a. 3; **b.** 2; **c.** 1

Language discovery 1

1 a. Guro snakker ikke kinesisk; **b.** Kommer dere ikke fra USA?; **c.** Du har ikke lyst på kake; **d.** Han kommer ikke fra Frankrike; **e.** Hvorfor er du ikke trøtt?; **f.** Har du ikke lyst til å gå tur?

2 a. 3; **b.** 4; **c.** 6; **d.** 2; **e.** 1; **f.** 7; **g.** 5; **h.** 10; **i.** 8; **j.** 9

Dialogue 2

1 She is not going to Norway

2 a. Isabel; **b.** David; **c.** Gordon; **d.** Ruth; **e.** Because she does not have time

Language discovery 2

1 ja and jo

2 nei

3 a. 1; **b.** 1; **c.** 1; **d.** 2

4 a. 1. Yes, I do; **2.** No, I don't.

b. 1. Yes, I have; **2.** No I haven't.

c. 1. Yes, she is; **2.** No, she isn't.

5 a. 1. Jo, det gjør han; **2.** Nei, det gjør han ikke.

b. 1. Jo, hun har det; **2.** Nei, hun har ikke det.

c. 1. Jo, det er han; **2.** Nei, det er han ikke.

Practice

2 a. He comes from Kristiansand; **b.** She comes from the USA; **c.** They live in Bergen; **d.** She is studying at university; **e.** She studies languages; **f.** They only speak English and Norwegian; **g.** She speaks English, Norwegian, French and Spanish

Test yourself

1 a. Hun snakker ikke spansk; **b.** Har du ikke lyst på pizza?; **c.** Han lærer seg ikke tysk; **d.** Jeg kommer ikke fra England; **e.** Har dere ikke lyst til å lære dere fransk?; **f.** Snakker du ikke norsk?; **g.** Kommer du ikke fra Australia?; **h.** Han snakker ikke arabisk; **i.** De drar ikke til Norge; **j.** Han heter ikke Walid.
2 a. Jeg bor ikke i Oslo nå. / Nå bor jeg ikke i Oslo; **b.** Bor du ikke i Bergen?; **c.** Hvorfor kommer du ikke?; **d.** Han kommer ikke fra USA; **e.** Jeg har ikke to katter.
3. (Possible answer) Stine og Haakon snakker om språk. Han sier han snakker norsk, fransk, tysk, engelsk og italiensk. Stine snakker også norsk, fransk, engelsk og litt tysk, men ikke italiensk. De snakker om hvor flinke folk er i språk og om vanskelige språk. Stine vil lære seg hindi og Haakon skal lære bort norsk og lære seg portugisisk.
4. (Possible answers) **a.** Jeg heter...; **b.** Jeg kommer fra...;
c. Jeg bor i...; **d.** Jeg snakker...; **e.** Jeg lærer meg norsk; **f.** Jeg har lyst til å...;
g. Jeg har lyst på...

UNIT 3

Discovery questions: førtifem, sekstisju, åttito

Vocabulary builder

1 before tens or units
2 a. femtiseks; **b.** åttini; **c.** nittisju; **d.** syttifire; **e.** tjuefem; **f.** trettitre; **g.** hundre og ti; **h.** fem hundre og sekstitre; **i.** seks tusen åtte hundre og nittisju; **j.** titusentrehundre og førtifem; **k.** førtitusenfemhundre og sekstisju; **l.** trehundrefemtisjutusenfemhundre

Dialogue 1

1 That they go to a café to have a cup of coffee and talk some more
2 a. She lived in Tøyen; **b.** She lives in Frogner; **c.** He lives in Vinderen; **d.** She is a teacher at university; **e.** He works in a bank
3 a. 2; **b.** 4; **c.** 1; **d.** 3
4 a. 2; **b.** 1; **c.** 3

Language discovery 1

1 a. i; **b.** fra; **c.** i; **d.** i; **e.** i; **f.** fra; **g.** på / i; **h.** i; **i.** på; **j.** på; **k.** på

Dialogue 2

1 Because he reads a lot
2 To the travel section
3 a. He is interested in many things; **b.** He likes to travel; **c.** They are on the second floor, next to the dictionaries.
4 a. 3; **b.** 4; **c.** 5; **d.** 1; **e.** 2
5 a. 1; **b.** 2; **c.** 2; **d.** 4; **e.** 1; **f.** 3

Language discovery 2

1 a. bilen; **b.** dagen; **c.** gutten; **d.** katten; **e.** vennen; **f.** pizzaen; **g.** læreren; **h.** mannen
2 a. biler; **b.** dager; **c.** gutter; **d.** katter; **e.** venner; **f.** pizzaer; **g.** lærere; **h.** menn; **i.** They become *lærere* and *menn,* instead of taking the final *-er.*
3 a. bilene; **b.** dagene; **c.** guttene; **d.** kattene; **e.** vennene; **f.** pizzaene; **g.** lærerne; **h.** mennene; **i.** They make the final *-ene* form from the indefinite plural form.
4 a. dama; **b.** jenta; **c.** kaka; **d.** lampa; **e.** skiva; **f.** venninna; **g.** boka; **h.** natta
5 a. damer; **b.** jenter; **c.** kaker; **d.** lamper; **e.** skiver; **f.** venninner; **g.** bøker; **h.** netter; **i.** As well as taking the *-er* ending, books and nights also change the vowel in the base word.
6 a. damene; **b.** jentene; **c.** kakene; **d.** lampene; **e.** skivene; **f.** venninnene; **g.** bøkene; **h.** nettene; **i.** As well as taking the *-ene* ending, they also change the vowel in the base word.
7 a. eplet; **b.** hotellet; **c.** vinduet; **d.** bordet; **e.** brødet; **f.** hjemmet; **g.** huset; **h.** kurset; **i.** rommet; **j.** skapet; **k.** They double the final consonant in the base form.
8 a. epler; **b.** hoteller; **c.** vinduer; **d.** bord; **e.** brød; **f.** hjem; **g.** hus; **h.** kurs; **i.** rom; **j.** skap; **k.** The majority don't change.
9 a. eplene; **b.** hotellene; **c.** vinduene; **d.** bordene; **e.** brødene; **f.** hjemmene; **g.** husene; **h.** kursene; **i.** rommene; **j.** skapene; **k.** They double the final consonant in the base form.
10 a. 1; **b.** 2; **c.** 2; **d.** 3
11 a. 4; **b.** 3; **c.** 2; **d.** 1

Practice

1 a. She has a total of eight pets (3 dogs, 2 cats, 1 horse, 2 parrots); **b.** three; **c.** two; **d.** two; **e.** one; **f.** a turtle
2 a. 2; **b.** 3; **c.** 1

Test yourself

1 a. De spiser mye brød; **b.** Han er 34 år gammel; **c.** Jeg har det travelt; **d.** Bøkene står i bokhylla; **e.** Hvor gammel er du?; **f.** Hun drikker mye kaffe; **g.** Flaska står på bordet.

2 a. Jeg snakker sju språk; **b.** Jeg har det travelt; **c.** Det er lenge siden sist; **d.** Katten står på skapet; **e.** Kan du komme til meg?; **f.** Kan jeg hjelpe deg?; **g.** Liker han krim?

3

Entall – *singular*		Flertall – *plural*		*English translation*
Ubestemt – *indeterminate*	Bestemt – *determinate*	Ubestemt – *indeterminate*	Bestemt – *determinate*	
en **barnehage**	barnehagen	barnehager	barnehagene	kindergarten
ei **bokhylle**	bokhylla	bokhyller	bokhyllene	bookshelf
ei **brødskive**	brødskiva	brødskiver	brødskivene	slice of bread
et **kjøleskap**	kjøleskapet	kjøleskap	kjøleskapene	fridge
et **nattbord**	nattbordet	nattbord	nattbordene	bedside table
et **pauserom**	pauserommet	pauserom	pauserommene	break room
et **skrivebord**	skrivebordet	skrivebord	skrivebordene	desk
et **spedbarn**	spedbarnet	spedbarn	spedbarna	infant
et **spisebord**	spisebordet	spisebord	spisebordene	dining table
et **spørsmål**	spørsmålet	spørsmål	spørsmålene	question
et **spørsmålstegn**	spørsmålstegnet	spørsmålstegn	spørsmålstegnene	question mark

REVIEW 1

1 Hei! Hyggelig å treffe deg! *Hi! Nice meeting you!*

1 a. 3; **b.** 1; **c.** 4; **d.** 6; **e.** 5; **f.** 2

2 a. Does she have a girlfriend?; **b.** Who are you?; **c.** When are you coming?; **d.** What is she doing here?; **e.** What are you studying?; **f.** Where do you study?

3 a. Hun heter Fatima; **b.** Jeg bor i Bergen, men jeg kommer fra Stavanger; **c.** Hva heter du?; **d.** Abby og Maja er venninner; **e.** Sven er student; **f.** Nora er lege.

4 a. 2; **b.** 4; **c.** 5; **d.** 6; **e.** 3; **f.** 1

5

Across: 1. hei; **2.** hva; **3.** hvordan; **4.** komme; **5.** takk; **6.** jobbe; **7.** fra; **8.** snakke

Down: 1. ha; **2.** det; **3.** bra

Hidden sentence: Ha det bra, which means take care.

2 Hvilket språk snakker du nå? *What language are you speaking now?*

1 a. jeg; **b.** jeg; **c.** han; **d.** han; **e.** vi; **f.** dere; **g.** vi; **h.** vi; **i.** dere; **j.** vi

2 a. What languages do you speak?; **b.** What language are you speaking?; **c.** Don't you come from Bristol?; **d.** I would like to learn Hindi; **e.** Yes, he lives in Stavanger; **f.** No, he doesn't; **g.** She studies languages.

3 a. Er du ikke norsk?; **b.** Bor du i Oslo?; **c.** Jeg bor ikke i Bergen nå. / Nå bor jeg ikke i Bergen; **d.** Jeg har lyst til å se på film; **e.** Jeg har lyst på sjokolade; **f.** Jeg snakker engelsk, norsk, italiensk, fransk, tysk, svensk og dansk.

4 a. Jeg heter...; **b.** Jeg bor i...; **c.** Jeg kommer fra...; **d.** Jeg snakker...; **e.** Jeg lærer meg norsk; **f.** Ja, det har jeg. / Nei, det har jeg ikke; **g.** Ja, det har jeg. / Nei, det har jeg ikke; **h.** Jo, det har jeg! / Nei, det har jeg ikke.

5

Across: 1. svensk; **2.** norsk; **3.** russisk; **4.** engelsk; **5.** italiensk

Down: (mystery word): Norge

3 Hvor mange bøker har du? *How many books do you have?*

1 a. på; **b.** på; **c.** i; **d.** i; **e.** til; **f.** til; **g.** fra; **h.** ved; **i.** om

2 a. to, en; **b.** fem; **c.** femtiåtte; **d.** sju; **e.** seks

3 a. Hvor mange språk snakker du?; **b.** Hvor mye brød spiser du **c.** Jeg spiser mye pizza; **d.** Hvor mange barn har du?; **e.** Jeg er 20 (år gammel); **f.** (Det er) lenge siden sist.

4 a. et eple; **b.** mannen; **c.** Kaka; **d.** venninne; **e.** Huset, byen; **f.** brød. **g.** katten, bordet

5

Across: 1. barn; **2.** bokhylle; **3.** gutt; **4.** dag; **5.** skrivebord; **6.** kvinne; **7.** katt; **8.** brødskive; **9.** spørsmålstegn; **10.** hund

Down: (mystery word) ryggsekken (*the backpack*)

UNIT 4

Discovery question: Great-great-grandparents, great-great-grandmother and great-great-grandfather

Dialogue 1

1 That there are three Norwegian words that mean cousin

2 a. They are sweethearts; **b.** They come from Tromsø; **c.** They are siblings; **d.** Tove is Johan's fiancée; **e.** They are cousins

3 a. 5; **b.** 3; **c.** 4; **d.** 6; **e.** 2; **f.** 1

4 a. 2; **b.** 1; **c.** 3; **d.** 3; **e.** 4; **f.** 1

Language discovery 1

1 a. broren; **b.** faren; **c.** fetteren; **d.** forelderen; **e.** nevøen; **f.** onkelen; **g.** svogeren; **h.** sønnen
2 a. brødre; **b.** fedre; **c.** fettere; **d.** foreldre; **e.** nevøer; **f.** onkler; **g.** svogere; **h.** sønner
3 a. brødrene; **b.** fedrene; **c.** fetterne; **d.** foreldrene; **e.** nevøene; **f.** onklene; **g.** svogerne; **h.** sønnene
4 a. dattera; **b.** kona; **c.** kusina; **d.** mora; **e.** niesa; **f.** svigerinna; **g.** søstera; **h.** tanta
5 a. døtre; **b.** koner; **c.** kusiner; **d.** mødre; **e.** nieser; **f.** svigerinner; **g.** søstre; **h.** tanter; **i.** They also change the vowel in the base form.
6 a. døtrene; **b.** konene; **c.** kusinene; **d.** mødrene; **e.** niesene; **f.** svigerinnene; **g.** søstrene; **h.** tantene; **i.** They also change the vowel in the base form.
7 a. barnet; **b.** barnebarnet; **c.** søskenet; **d.** søskenbarnet; **e.** bonusbarnet
8 a. barn; **b.** barnebarn; **c.** søsken; **d.** søskenbarn
9 a. barna; **b.** barnebarna; **c.** søsknene; **d.** søskenbarna; **e.** It exchanges *-en-* with *-ne-* in the center of the word.
10 a. Jentene leker; **b.** Barna sover; **c.** Hun har et barn; **d.** Mora synger; **e.** Fedrene snakker; **f.** Dette er min bestemor; **g.** Jeg har en onkel og ei tante; **h.** De har tre bonusbarn.
11 a. bror; **b.** hus; **c.** stesønn; **d.** dattera; **e.** hunden
12 a. 5; **b.** 4; **c.** 2; **d.** 6; **e.** 1; **f.** 3
13 a. hit; **b.** der; **c.** her; **d.** dit; **e.** hit; **f.** der; **g.** her; **h.** dit

Dialogue 2

1 Two
2 a. Seven; **b.** One; **c.** Six; **d.** Five; **e.** Five; **f.** One
3 a. 2; **b.** 5; **c.** 7; **d.** 4; **e.** 6; **f.** 1; **g.** 3
4 a. 2; **b.** 3; **c.** 4; **d.** 1
5 a. 27; **b.** Sin, sitt, sine, min, mitt, mine, din, ditt, dine, deres, vår, vårt, våre

Language discovery 2

1 a. My parents are coming; **b.** My sister's name is Astrid; **c.** Siri is your sister-in-law; **d.** My grandfather Arthur is coming with his wife; **e.** My aunts and uncles also are coming with their children and grandchildren; **f.** Aunt Gunhild and her husband, Aleksander, are coming with their three sons; **g.** And then Uncle Frode is coming with his wife Merete, and their four children; **h.** Mum's sister is coming with her partner, Aunt Bergljot; **i.** Our family is rather big; **j.** My mother has only one sister; **k.** Aunt Siobhán and her partner Leroy are expecting their first child now; **l.** It's my responsibility, not yours!

2 a. 1, 4; **b.** 2, 4; **c.** 1, 4
3 a. 2; **b.** 5; **c.** 1; **d.** 6; **e.** 4; **f.** 3

Practice

1 a. their families; **b.** four; **c.** No, she has a twin sister; **d.** Yes, she does; **e.** They're coming to visit her in Norway; **f.** Yes, she is.

Test yourself

1 a. Jeg har ei stesøster / bonussøster og to brødre.; **b.** Hun er tanta mi. / Hun er min tante; **c.** Min onkel har to barn; **d.** Hennes bestefar er 98 år gammel. / Bestefaren hennes er 98 år gammel; **e.** Hans kone heter Astrid. / Kona hans heter Astrid; **f.** Kusina mi er 20 år gammel. / Min kusine er 20 år gammel.
2 a. Hvor gammel er hun?; **b.** Hva er forskjellen mellom kusine og fetter?; **c.** Min mor heter Laura; **d.** Ola er broren til Gudrun og kommer fra Tromsø.
3 *Personal answers beginning with:* jeg har ...

UNIT 5

Discovery questions: a. they are both plural adjectives; **b.** They are plural, because they end in *-e*.

Vocabulary builder

Clothes

bluse (ei)	*blouse*
hatt (en)	*hat*
jakke (ei)	*jacket*
sokk (en)	*sock*
t-skjorte (ei)	*T-shirt*

Colors

blå	*blue*
grønn	*green*
grå	*gray*
rød	*red*

Dialogue 1

1 A beret
2 It costs 299 nok.
3 a. At a clothes shop. **b.** Because she has a new pair; **c.** They are down there.
4 a. 2; **b.** 5; **c.** 3; **d.** 1; **e.** 4

5 a. 2; **b.** 3; **c.** 1
6 a. 2; **b.** 3; **c.** 1

Language discovery 1

1 a. Vi må kjøpe noe; **b.** Jeg vil (gjerne) kjøpe noe for meg selv; **c.** Jeg bør prøve det; **d.** Skal vi kjøpe henne en genser?
2 a. 5; **b.** 1; **c.** 4; **d.** 6; **e.** 7; **f.** 2; **g.** 3

Dialogue 2

1 Going to a concert
2 Yes
3 a. If she wants to join them; **b.** Yes; **c.** That she has to work
4 a. 2; **b.** 3; **c.** 4; **d.** 1
5 a. 3; **b.** 1/4; **c.** 4/1; **d.** 3; **e.** 1; **f.** 2

Language discovery 2

1 a. 8; **b.** 12; **c.** 9; **d.** 2; **e.** 4; **f.** 6; **g.** 7; **h.** 11; **i.** 10; **j.** 1; **k.** 5; **l.** 3
2 a. fint; **b.** rødt; **c.** grønt
3 a. nytt; **b.** blått
4 a. 10; **b.** 6; **c.** 9; **d.** 5; **e.** 8; **f.** 4; **g.** 7; **h.** 1; **i.** 3; **j.** 2
5 a. 2; **b.** 1; **c.** 2; **d.** 1
6 a. 1; **b.** 2; **c.** 1; **d.** 2; **e.** 1; **f.** 2; **g.** 1; **h.** 2; **i.** 2

Practice

1 a. Jeg har på meg...; **b.** Jeg er veldig glad i å bruke skjørt; **c.** Jeg liker...; **d.** Jeg hater...; **e.** lyse and mørke
2 a. a T-shirt, a sweater, a skirt, tights, shoes, a jacket, gloves and a scarf; **b.** light blue, dark grey, green, black, red, and lilac; **c.** She likes both light and dark colours, but says that sometimes dark colours can be boring; **d.** She hates wearing high-heeled shoes; **e.** She likes them.
3 a. ung; **b.** gammel, smart / flink, flink / smart; **c.** stor, liten; **d.** hvit, stort; **e.** pen / solrik, solrik / pen, koselig; **f.** hyggelige, snill / morsom, morsom / snill; **g.** fantastisk

Test yourself

1 a. Ei dyr jakke; **b.** Et blått skjerf; **c.** Den smarte jent; **d.** grønne hansker/ votter; **e.** en billig genser; **f.** Den snille gutten.
2 a. bør / må; **b.** skal / vil / må; **c.** skal; **d.** kan / vil; **e.** vil / kan / skal
4 a. I dag har jeg på meg en lyseblå t-skjorte; **b.** Så har jeg på meg ei rød jakke; **c.** Nå bor jeg i Oslo; **d.** Nå bor Hans ikke i Stavanger.

UNIT 6

Discovery question: a. 16.10 / 04.10; **b.** We're meeting at 14.30.

Vocabulary builder

å drikke	*to drink*
å fly	*to fly*
å komme	*to come*
å ligge	*to lie (down)*
å sitte	*to sit*
å ta	*to take*

Dialogue 1

1 She gets up at 06.45, he gets up at 07.30.
2 He walks; she walks, then takes the tube and the bus.
3 a. At 9; **b.** He likes to sleep until late; **c.** Because she has to buy a new car; **d.** She goes home, changes clothes, and buys groceries. She goes to the German course once a week and sometimes she meets her friends and goes to bed early; **e.** He takes a walk in the woods, then he goes home and makes dinner. Sometimes he invites some friends to dinner. After dinner he watches TV, or listens to music while he reads a book. He doesn't like going to bed early.
4 a. 2; **b.** 5; **c.** 4; **d.** 1; **e.** 3
5 a. 3; **b.** 1; **c.** 3; **d.** 3; **e.** 4; **f.** 4; **g.**1; **h.** 2
6 a. 2; **b.** 4; **c.** 3; **d.** 1

Language discovery 1

1 a. Først, så / etterpå; **b.** Først, etterpå / så; **c.** etter; **d.** Etterpå; **e.** Etter, så, Etterpå
2 a. seg; **b.** seg; **c.** meg; **d.** dere; **e.** seg; **f.** deg; **g.** dere; **h.** meg; **i.** seg; **j.** deg

Dialogue 2

1 At 12:15
2 Because Astrid is finished later (at 12)
3 a. In front of the library; **b.** He will take the tram; **c.** At 12; **d.** At 12.15
4 a. 5; **b.** 7; **c.** 6; **d.** 8; **e.** 3; **f.** 1; **g.** 4; **h.** 2
5 a. 3; **b.** 4; **c.** 1; **d.** 3; **e.** 1; **f.** 3

Language discovery 2

1 a. sitter, ser; **b.** ligger, leser; **c.** står, snakker; **d.** sitter, venter; **e.** går, ser; **f.** ligger, sover; **g.** står, snakker

2 a. hjemme; **b.** hjem; **c.** inne; **d.** inn; **e.** ute; **f.** ut; **g.** nede; **h.** ned; **i.** oppe; **j.** opp

Practice

1 a. Hver dag; **b.** aldri; **c.** ofte; **d.** alltid; **e.** noen ganger

2 a. 1; **b.** 3; **c.** 1; **d.** 3

4 a. Jeg legger meg tidlig; **b.** Barnet ønsker seg en hund; **c.** De har ikke bestemt seg; **d.** Magnus står og venter på bussen; **e.** Barnet ligger og sover.

Test yourself

1 a. Først spiser jeg frokost, så går jeg på jobb; **b.** Jeg tar bussen til jobb; **c.** Etter jobb, går jeg på tyskkurs; **d.** Vi sees. / Vi ses; **e.** Først handler jeg mat, så går jeg hjem og leser ei bok; **f.** Jeg står her og venter på deg.

2 a. sitter / står; **b.** står / sitter; **c.** drar; **d.** står / sitter; **e.** går

4 a. Jeg vekker deg; **b.** Jeg bor langt fra min jobb; **c.** Jeg liker å sove lenge om morgenen; **d.** Etter jobb tar jeg en tur i skogen; **e.** Først dusjer jeg, så spiser jeg frokost. / Først spiser jeg frokost, så dusker jeg; **f.** Jeg trenger å konsentrere meg.

REVIEW 2

4 Dette er familien min *This is my family*

1 a. 14; **b.** 7; **c.** 10; **d.** 9; **e.** 13; **f.** 3; **g.** 5; **h.** 6; **i.** 11; **j.** 12; **k.** 4; **l.** 8; **m.** 1; **n.** 2

2 a. What does it mean?; **b.** How do you say 'fiancé' in Norwegian?; **c.** It's very difficult to remember everything; **d.** Mum's sister is Sigrid; **e.** It's going to be cosy.

3 a. Søstera mi heter Astrid; **b.** Stebroren hans heter Ciarán; **c.** Søstera hans heter Siobhán; **d.** Nå forstår jeg!; **e.** Hva heter Toves forlovede?; **f.** Hva mener du?

4 a. min; **b.** hans; **c.** hennes; **d.** sitt; **e.** deres; **f.** sin; **g.** sin; **h.** di

5

Across: 1. barnebarn; **2.** svigerfar; **3.** sønn; **4.** datter; **5.** onkel; **6.** mødre; **7.** tippoldefar; **8.** søster

Down: (mystery word) bestemor

5 Vi skal handle! *We're going shopping!*

1 a. 3; **b.** 10; **c.** 8; **d.** 7; **e.** 1; **f.** 9; **g.** 5; **h.** 2; **i.** 4; **j.** 6

2 a. I would like to buy a new sweater; **b.** Guro cannot come today; **c.** You should study Norwegian; **d.** He's going to Rome next summer; **e.** Are you

going to buy this book?; **f.** Do you want to meet him?; **g.** Can Frode help you?; **h.** I have to go now; **i.** I should go now.
3 a. Hun har på seg blå sko; **b.** Jeg bor i et lite hus; **c.** Han har tre små barn; **d.** Du har en rød bil; **e.** Vennene mine er morsomme; **f.** Dette er et koselig rom.
4 a. 6; **b.** 9; **c.** 10; **d.** 11; **e.** 12; **f.** 15; **g.** 5; **h.** 14; **i.** 7; **j.** 13; **k.** 2; **l.** 8; **m.** 1; **n.** 4; **o.** 3

5
Across: 1. bukse; **2.** skjorte; **3.** strømpebukse; **4.** slips; **5.** undertøy; **6.** badedrakt; **7.** genser; **8.** votter; **9.** miniskjørt; **10.** sokk
Down: (mystery word) bobledress

6 Hva gjør du hver dag? *What do you do every day?*
1 a. Klokka er / Den er kvart over tolv; **b.** Klokka er / Den er kvart på seks; **c.** Klokka er / Den er halv tolv; **d.** Klokka er / Den er ti over ti; **e.** Klokka er / Den er fem over åtte; **f.** Klokka er / Den er ti på halv fem; **g.** Klokka er / Den er fem på halv fire; **h.** Klokka er / Den er ti over halv sju; **i.** Klokka er / Den er fem over halv fire
2 a. I go to bed early; **b.** I'm late; **c.** I like to sleep until late; **d.** How long does it take?; **e.** What do you do in the morning?; **f.** Almost one hour; **g.** I have to buy a new car; **h.** After work I take a walk in the woods; **i.** We can meet in front of the library; **j.** When will you be done?
3 a. Jeg står opp; **b.** Hvor lang tid tar det?; **c.** Før frokost tar jeg en dusj; **d.** Jeg våkner opp; **e.** Jeg har en hatt på meg; **f.** Jeg liker å sove lenge; **g.** Jeg har ei jakke på meg; **h.** Først dusjer jeg, så spiser jeg frokost.
4 a. seg; **b.** meg; **c.** meg; **d.** deg; **e.** seg; **f.** seg; **g.** deg; **h.** seg; **i.** deg

5
Across: 1. bli; **2.** sitte; **3.** gå; **4.** gjøre; **5.** komme
Down: (mystery word) ligge

UNIT 7
Discovery question: moose burger

Vocabulary builder
FRUKT *Fruit*

banan	*banana*
eple	*apple*
aprikos	*apricot*

blåbær	*blueberry*
aubergine	*aubergine*
potet	*potato*
spinat	*spinach*
squash	*squash*
tomat	*tomato*

DRIKKE *Drinks*

juice	*juice*
melk	*milk*
vin	*wine*

Dialogue 1

1 No
2 Sesame seeds and nuts
3 a. She buys four rolls; **b.** She buys a piece of carrot cake and a piece of apple pie; **c.** Two wheat buns, two raisin buns and a 'school bun'; **d.** She decides to eat a sandwich with salmon and eggs; **e.** She drinks some orange juice and a cup of coffee; **f.** She pays 259 nok.
4 a. 5; **b.** 3; **c.** 4; **d.** 2; **e.** 6; **f.** 1
5 a. 4; **b.** 3; **c.** 1; **d.** 2

Language discovery 1

1 a. 6; **b.** 4; **c.** 5; **d.** 7; **e.** 8; **f.** 1; **g.** 2; **h.** 3; **i.** 10; **j.** 11; **k.** 9

Dialogue 2

1 No
2 No
3 a. beef, carrots, rutabaga and root parsley; **b.** pepper, butter, potatoes and broth; **c.** Yes; **d.** MatPrat; **e.** Literally it means 'food talk'.
4 a. 2; **b.** 4; **c.** 1; **d.** 3
5 a. 3; **b.** 1; **c.** 3; **d.** 2; **e.** 2; **f.** 3; **g.** 4
6 a. 3; **b.** 2; **c.** 4; **d.** 1
7 a. 1; **b.** 3; **c.** 2

Language discovery 2

1 a. 1; **b.** 1; **c.** 1; **d.** 2; **e.** 1; **f.** 2; **g.** 1; **h.** 1
2 a. å skjære; **b.** å ha; **c.** å vente; **d.** å brune; **e.** å helle; **f.** å tilsette; **g.** å la; **h.** å røre; **i.** å se; **j.** å smake; **k.** å servere
3 a. 3; **b.** 1; **c.** 2; **d.** 3; **e.** 3; **f.** 3; **g.** 2; **h.** 2

Practice

2 a. 18; **b.** 22; **c.** Indian or Mexican food; **d.** No

3 a. Jeg gleder meg til i kveld; **b.** meksikansk frister; **c.** Jeg tar meg en liten pause for å planlegge kvelden.

Test yourself

2 a. Jeg vil gjerne bestille et bord på restaurant; **b.** Rekker vi konserten klokka 22?; **c.** Jeg har litt lyst på indisk mat; **d.** Hva synes du?; **e.** Spiser de med oss?; **f.** Jeg gleder meg til i kveld!

4 a. Jeg vil gjerne ha kjøttboller med ertestuing, poteter, brun saus, tyttebærsyltetøy og en øl.

b. Jeg vil gjerne ha en kanelbolle, et glass kald melk og en kopp kaffe.

c. Jeg er allergisk mot...

d. Jeg er vegetarianer; Jeg spiser ikke kjøtt og fisk (*I don't eat meat and fish*).

UNIT 8

Discovery question: hostel

Dialogue 1

1 No

2 Yes

3 a. To Bryggen; **b.** Near Bergenhus Festning; **c.** Julehuset (Christmas shop); **d.** The fish market; **e.** The following day, when it should be sunny

4 a. 3; **b.** 5; **c.** 4; **d.** 6; **e.** 2; **f.** 1

5 a. 3; **b.** 4; **c.** 1; **d.** 2; **e.** 4; **f.** 1

Language discovery 1

1 a. til venstre; **b.** til høyre; **c.** rett fram; **d.** blant; **e.** bak; **f.** foran; **g.** under; **h.** utenfor; **i.** over; **j.** ved siden av; **k.** i nærheten av; **l.** til venstre for; **m.** til høyre for; **n.** mellom

Dialogue 2

1 Presents for family and friends, something Norwegian to take home and postcards

2 To the travel agency

3 a. In the vicinity of the travel agency; **b.** The post office; **c.** 15; **d.** 1,494 nok total; **e.** A triple room; **f.** 2,190 nok, including breakfast; **g.** Three days

4 a. 7; **b.** 5; **c.** 1; **d.** 6; **e.** 3; **f.** 4; **g.** 2

5 a. 2; **b.** 3; **c.** 2; **d.** 3; **e.** 1; **f.** 1; **g.** 2; **h.** 3; **i.** 1

Practice

På reisebyrå ...

Selgeren	Hei, hva kan jeg hjelpe dere med?
Maja	Hei, vi trenger å bestille togbilletter til Lillehammer.
Selgeren	Hvor mange trenger dere og når vil dere reise?
Maja	Vi er tre og vi vil gjerne reise tidlig i morgen.
Selgeren	Trenger dere tur-retur?
Maja	Ja, takk. Vi tenker å reise tilbake sent på søndag.
Selgeren	Det blir 1494 kroner til sammen. Toget går på fredag kl. 7 og dere kommer tilbake på søndag kl. 22.
Maja	Fantastisk! Kan du bestille overnatting også?
Selgeren	Selvfølgelig. Hvor vil dere bo? Skal jeg se etter et dobbeltrom og et enkeltrom?
Maja	Vi har ikke råd til noe kjempedyrt. Så et tremannsrom kan være fint.
Selgeren	Jeg ser på vandrerhjemmet først da ... ja, de har et tremannsrom ledig til 2190 kroner inkludert frokost.
Maja	Fantastisk, vi tar det. Er wifi gratis?
Selgeren	Ja, det er det.
Maja	Supert! Kan jeg betale med kort?
Selgeren	Ja, det kan du.

2 a. weak and cold; **b.** everywhere; **c.** he thinks so
3 a. 5; **b.** 4; **c.** 2; **d.** 1; **e.** 6; **f.** 3

Test yourself

2 a. Herifra må dere gå langs veien mot nord; **b.** Da tar dere til venstre; **c.** Så tar dere veien til høyre; **d.** Dere tar til venstre etter 200 meter; **e.** Etter 100 meter tar dere til høyre; **f.** Etter 15 meter går dere rett fram.
4 Jeg har bursdag den... / Bursdagen min er den... / Min bursdag er den... / Jeg ble født den...

UNIT 9

Discovery question: God påske

Vocabulary builder

å gjøre	*to do*
å glemme	*to forget*
å gå	*to walk / go*

å ha	*to have*
å hate	*to hate*
å høre	*to hear*
å jobbe	*to work*
å lage	*to make*
å leie	*to rent*
å lese	*to read*
å nå	*to reach*
å se	*to see*
å si	*to say*
å skjønne	*to understand*
å snakke	*to speak*
å spille	*to play*
å spise	*to eat*
å sy	*to sew*
å tro	*to believe*
å vente	*to wait*

Dialogue 1

1 She was wearing a *bunad*.

2 Because her *bunad* was at her parents' house.

3 a. With some friends; **b.** To Karl Johans gate; **c.** She ate ice cream with her niece; **d.** Soft serve; **e.** Hot dog; **f.** To the rollercoasters in Grønland

4 a. 5; **b.** 4; **c.** 6; **d.** 3; **e.** 2; **f.** 1

5 a. 4; **b.** 2; **c.** 1; **d.** 2; **e.** 2; **f.** 3; **g.** 4

Language discovery 1

1 a. snakket; **b.** hatet; **c.** ventet

2 a. leste; **b.** hørte; **c.** spilte; **d.** glemte

3 a. lagde; **b.** leide; **c.** bøyde

4 a. hadde; **b.** trodde; **c.** nådde; **d.** sydde

Dialogue 2

1 Germany

2 Australia and New Zealand

3 a. 8; **b.** Australia, New Zealand, Canada, USA, Austria, France, Italy and Spain; **c.** 2; **d.** Germany and Spain; **e.** That they will travel together to a place neither of them has visited before

4 a. 3; **b.** 5; **c.** 1; **d.** 2; **e.** 4

5 a. 2; **b.** 1; **c.** 3; **d.** 4; **e.** 3

Language discovery 2
1 a. snakket; **b.** jobbet; **c.** ventet
2 a. lest; **b.** hørt; **c.** spilt; **d.** glemt
3 a. lagd; **b.** leid; **c.** bøyd
4 a. sydd; **b.** trodd; **c.** nådd; **d.** hatt

Practice
1 a. 1,80 m; **b.** blond; **c.** red; **d.** their baby; **e.** light blue
2 a. 1,80 meter høy; **b.** blondt hår; **c.** rødt hår; **d.** blå øyne; **e.** Vi ser frem til å treffe deg.

Test yourself
2 a. Vi ser frem til å treffe deg; **b.** Hurra for deg som fyller ditt år; **c.** Hva gjorde du etter toget?; **d.** Ja, men det var fullt av folk; **e.** Neste gang reiser jeg til Australia og New Zealand; **f.** Jeg har vært i Spania.
3 a. drakk; **b.** forsto; **c.** gjorde, sa; **d.** Var
4 a. har drukket; **b.** har forstått; **c.** har gjort; **d.** har blitt / har vært; **e.** har vært

UNIT 10
Discovery question: a. whales; **b.** seals

Vocabulary builder

varmt	*warm*
kaldt	*cold*
regn	*rain*
sol	*sun*
vind	*wind*
å regne	*to rain*
å snø	*to snow*
å tordne	*to thunder*
å lyne	*to strike with lightning*
å svette	*to sweat*
å fryse	*to freeze*
å skinne	*to shine*

1 a. 4; **b.** 3; **c.** 5; **d.** 1; **e.** 2

Dialogue 1
1 Ice skating
2 Goes skiing and takes walks in the woods
3 a. Yes; **b.** Spring; **c.** He travels south; **d.** South

4 a. 2; **b.** 5; **c.** 1; **d.** 6; **e.** 3; **f.** 4
5 a. 2; **b.** 1; **c.** 4; **d.** 5; **e.** 3; **f.** 2; **g.** 1; **h.** 3; **i.** 4; **j.** 5
6 a. Det er koselig å være hjemme om vinteren. / Om vinteren er det koselig å være hjemme; **b.** Jeg går på ski om vinteren. / Om vinteren går jeg på ski; **c.** Jeg liker best å reise til varme steder om vinteren. / Om vinteren liker jeg best å reise il varme steder; **d.** Jeg går lange turer i skogen om sommeren. / Om sommeren går jeg lange turer i skogen; **e.** Været er pent og det er blomster overalt om våren / Om våren er været pent og det er blomster overalt; **f.** Jeg reiser ofte til Syden og nyter sola på stranda om høsten. / Om høsten reiser jeg ofte til Syden og nyter sola på stranda.

Language discovery 1
1 a. 1; **b.** 5; **c.** 6; **d.** 2; **e.** 7; **f.** 4; **g.** 3; **h.** 8
2 a. 3; **b.** 2; **c.** 2; **d.** 2; **e.** 1; **f.** 3; **g.** 3; **h.** 2
3 a. Yesterday; **b.** A day; **c.** This morning; **d.** Last year; **e.** In October; **f.** Today; **g.** This summer; **h.** Tomorrow; **i.** In the summer; **j.** Next year; **k.** In the winter; **l.** This Christmas; **m.** This Easter; **n.** A season

Dialogue 2
1 Read, listen to music, take walks, play board games and computer games
2 Read, listen to music, take walks, play board games and computer games
3 a. Play games; **b.** Fairy tales from different lands; **c.** Because he is interested in Nordic literature and culture; **d.** That maybe she will read it too
4 a. 4; **b.** 3; **c.** 2; **d.** 5; **e.** 1
5 a. 2; **b.** 2; **c.** 2; **d.** 3; **e.** 4; **f.** 1; **g.** 4

Language discovery 2
1 a. kaldere; **b.** nyere
2 a. yngre; **b.** vakrere; **c.** morsommere; **d.** tyngre
3 a. billigst; **b.** dyrest; **c.** enklest; **d.** penest
4 a. yngst; **b.** vakrest; **c.** tyngst
5 a. mer; **b.** mest
6 a. bra; **b.** bedre; **c.** best; **d.** mange; **e.** flere; **f.** flest
7 a. 3; **b.** 2; **c.** 14; **d.** 5; **e.** 6; **f.** 4; **g.** 13; **h.** 7; **i.** 1; **j.** 9; **k.** 10; **l.** 11; **m.** 8; **n.** 12; **o.** 15

Practice

Marit	Å, jeg fryser, det er så kaldt!
Kristian	Ja, du har rett, men jeg liker når det er vinter og det snør.
Marit	Ja da, jeg liker også snøen og det er koselig å være hjemme om vinteren, men jeg liker ikke at det er mørkt.
Kristian	Hva gjør du vanligvis om vinteren?
Marit	Om vinteren går jeg på ski, men jeg liker best å gå på skøyter. Og så drar jeg på hyttetur, selvfølgelig! Hva med deg?
Kristian	Jeg går mye på ski, men jeg går også tur i skogen når det er snø. Hvilken årstid liker du best?
Marit	Jeg liker våren best, været blir pent og det er blomster overalt. Hva med deg?
Kristian	Jeg liker sommeren veldig godt.
Marit	Hva gjør du vanligvis om sommeren?
Kristian	Jeg reiser ofte til Syden og nyter sola/solen på stranda/stranden.
Marit	Å, det er nydelig! Jeg reiser også, men liker best å reise til varme steder om vinteren.
Kristian	Jeg skjønner. Det er også smart.
Marit	Ja, det er fint å ta en pause fra is og snø.

2 a. In Oxford; **b.** A class trip to London; **c.** Madame Tussaud's; **d.** Basketball, volleyball, cricket, tennis, swimming; **e.** Swimming
3 a. Jeg trives veldig godt her; **b.** Liknende; **c.** trøtte; **d.** Lillebror; **e.** Svømmehallen; **f.** Favoritt; **g.** Klemmer; **h.** Fortsatt; **i.** Masse

Test yourself
2 a. I dag er det veldig kaldt; **b.** Hun har nettopp dratt; **c.** Han har vært på ferie i en måned; **d.** Hun bodde i Norge for tre år siden; **e.** Når du kom hjem, var jeg ute.

REVIEW 3
7 Vi skal ut og spise *We're going out to eat*
1 a. 9; **b.** 10; **c.** 7; **d.** 6; **e.** 11; **f.** 8; **g.** 13; **h.** 2; **i.** 4; **j.** 12; **k.** 1; **l.** 3; **m.** 5
2 a. I think so; **b.** Would you like something to drink?; **c.** Are you ready to order?; **d.** What would you like to drink?; **e.** Would you like anything else?; **f.** This child's name is Hans; **g.** Add salt and pepper to taste; **h.** I don't eat food that comes from animals, I'm a vegan.

3 a. Smaker det godt?; **b.** Hva vil du ha?; **c.** Vil du ha noe annet?; **d.** Vil du ha noe å drikke?; **e.** Vil dere bestille?; **f.** Skjær kjøtt i terninger; **g.** Tilsett potet; **h.** Server med grovt brød.
4 a. Kom; **b.** Snakk; **c.** Skriv; **d.** Tilsett; **e.** Gå; **f.** la; **g.** Ring; **h.** Spis

5
Across: 1. brød; **2.** smør; **3.** gulrøtter; **4.** hasselnøtter; **5.** tomat; **6.** blåbærsyltetøy; **7.** hvitløk
Down: (mystery word) brunost

8 På ferie i Norge *On holiday in Norway*
1 a. Where is the museum?; **b.** Where is the hospital?; **c.** I have a bellyache; **d.** I have a sore throat; **e.** Go straight ahead; **f.** I would really like to see the Christmas house!; **g.** I think it's a good idea; **h.** Where do you want to stay?; **i.** I'm cold/freezing.
2 a. Hvor ligger suvenirbutikken?; **b.** Hvor mye koster billettene?; **c.** Hvor lenge blir dere?; **d.** Hvor kan vi spise?; **e.** Kan du være så snill å hjelpe meg?; **f.** Jeg er syk; **g.** Jeg vil bestille rommet på nettet; **h.** Jeg kjøper togbilletten i appen.
4
Across: 1. hals; **2.** hode; **3.** skulder; **4.** nese; **5.** pekefinger; **6.** kinn; **7.** nakke; **8.** albue
Down: (mystery word) hodepine

9 Snakk om fortiden *Talk about the past*
1 a. 2; **b.** 4; **c.** 9; **d.** 1; **e.** 3; **f.** 5; **g.** 6; **h.** 7; **i.** 8
2 a. She was very proud of her *bunad*.; **b.** What did you do after the parade?; **c.** It's a pity we didn't see each other; **d.** It was crowded; **e.** He forgot the keys at home this morning; **f.** I made a cake for her birthday.
3 a. Jeg drakk te i går; **b.** Var du hjemme i går?; **c.** Jeg snakket med Pål for tre dager siden; **d.** Han ventet på henne på kafeen; **e.** Hun hadde mange venner; **f.** Han nådde ikke flyplassen i tide; **g.** Hun har ikke gjort det jeg sa; **h.** Vi har ventet på dem i en time; **i.** Jeg har lagd ei kake; **j.** Jeg har aldri trodd på ham.
4 a. har trodd; **b.** forsto; **c.** har lest; **d.** gjorde; **e.** har hatt; **f.** Var; **g.** hatet; **h.** har lagd; **i.** leste; **j.** har spilt; **k.** hørte; **l.** trodde; **m.** har drukket; **n.** hadde; **o.** har ventet

5

Across: 1. spiste; **2.** drakk; **3.** lagde; **4.** jobbet; **5.** hatet; **6.** trodde; **7.** gikk; **8.** leste; **9.** glemte
Down: (mystery word) preteritum

10 Hva gjør du når du har fri? *What do you do in your free time?*

1 a. 5; **b.** 9; **c.** 7; **d.** 1; **e.** 10; **f.** 2; **g.** 3; **h.** 4; **i.** 6; **j.** 8
2 a. It's warm; **b.** The weather is nice; **c.** The weather is bad; **d.** There's thunder and lightning; **e.** It's snowing; **f.** It's hailing; **g.** It's 15 degrees below zero.
3 a. Sola skinner; **b.** Det er kaldt; **c.** Det er tåke; **d.** Det regner; **e.** Det blåser; **f.** Det er is; **g.** Jeg fryser; **h.** Jeg er varm; **i.** Jeg svetter.
4 a. mer; **b.** mange, forskjellige; **c.** veldig interessant; **d.** kaldere; **e.** yngre; **f.** dyrest; **g.** vakrest; **h.** mest praktisk; **i.** bedre; **j.** flere; **k.** dyreste; **l.** snilleste; **m.** peneste

5

Across: 1. spennende; **2.** kjedelig; **3.** kald; **4.** rotete; **5.** morsom; **6.** pen; **7.** varm; **8.** ekte; **9.** norsk; **10.** dyr; **11.** fersk
Down: (mystery word) sjarmerende

Grammar appendix

Nouns

Hankjønn – *masculine*			
Entall – *singular*			
Ubestemt – *indeterminate*		**Bestemt** – *determinate*	
en bil	*a car*	**bilen**	*the car*
en by	*a city*	**byen**	*the city*
en dag	*a day*	**dagen**	*the day*
en gutt	*a boy*	**gutten**	*the boy*
en hund	*a dog*	**hunden**	*the dog*
en katt	*a cat*	**katten**	*the cat*
en kollega	*a colleague*	**kollegaen**	*the colleague*
en kveld	*an evening*	**kvelden**	*the evening*
en kvinne	*a woman*	**kvinnen**	*the woman*
en pasta	*pasta*	**pastaen**	*the pasta*
en pizza	*a pizza*	**pizzaen**	*the pizza*
en skole	*a school*	**skolen**	*the school*
en sofa	*a sofa*	**sofaen**	*the sofa*
en stemme	*a voice*	**stemmen**	*the voice*
en trikk	*a tram*	**trikken**	*the tram*
en venn	*a friend*	**vennen**	*the friend*
en lærer	*a teacher*	**læreren**	*the teacher*
en mann	*a man*	**mannen**	*the man*
Flertall – *plural*			
Ubestemt – *indeterminate*		**Bestemt** – *determinate*	
biler	*(some) cars*	**bilene**	*the cars*
byer	*(some) cities*	**byene**	*the cities*
dager	*(some) days*	**dagene**	*the days*
gutter	*(some) boys*	**guttene**	*the boys*
hunder	*(some) dogs*	**hundene**	*the dogs*
katter	*(some) cats*	**kattene**	*the cats*
kollegaer	*(some) colleagues*	**kollegaene**	*the colleagues*
kvelder	*(some) evenings*	**kveldene**	*the evenings*
kvinner	*(some) women*	**kvinnene**	*the women*
pastaer	*(some) pasta*	**pastaene**	*the pasta*
pizzaer	*(some) pizzas*	**pizzaene**	*the pizzas*
skoler	*(some) schools*	**skolene**	*the schools*
sofaer	*(some) sofas*	**sofaene**	*the sofas*
stemmer	*(some) voices*	**stemmene**	*the voices*

Hankjønn – *masculine*			
trikker	*(some) trams*	**trikkene**	*the trams*
venner	*(some) friends*	**vennene**	*the friends*
lærere	*(some) teachers*	**lærerne**	*the teachers*
menn	*(some) men*	**mennene**	*the men*

Hunkjønn – *feminine*			
Entall – *singular*			
Ubestemt – *indeterminate*		**Bestemt** – *determinate*	
ei dame	*a woman*	**dama**	*the woman*
ei hylle	*a shelf*	**hylla**	*the shelf*
ei jente	*a girl*	**jenta**	*the girl*
ei kake	*a cake*	**kaka**	*the cake*
ei kvinne	*a woman*	**kvinna**	*the woman*
ei lampe	*a lamp*	**lampa**	*the lamp*
ei skive	*a slice*	**skiva**	*the slice*
ei sol	*a sun*	**sola**	*the sun*
ei venninne	*a (female) friend*	**venninna**	*the (female) friend*
ei bok	*a book*	**boka**	*the book*
ei natt	*a night*	**natta**	*the night*
Flertall – *plural*			
Ubestemt – *indeterminate*		**Bestemt** – *determinate*	
damer	*(some) women*	**damene**	*the women*
hyller	*(some) shelves*	**hyllene**	*the shelves*
jenter	*(some) girls*	**jentene**	*the girls*
kaker	*(some) cakes*	**kakene**	*the cakes*
kvinner	*(some) women*	**kvinnene**	*the women*
lamper	*(some) lamps*	**lampene**	*the lamps*
skiver	*(some) slices*	**skivene**	*the slices*
soler	*(some) suns*	**solene**	*the suns*
venninner	*(some female) friends*	**venninnene**	*the (female) friends*
bøker	*(some) books*	**bøkene**	*the books*
netter	*(some) nights*	**nettene**	*the nights*

Intetkjønn – *neuter*			
Entall – *singular*			
Ubestemt – *indeterminate*		**Bestemt** – *determinate*	
et eple	*an apple*	**eplet**	*the apple*
et hotell	*a hotel*	**hotellet**	*the hotel*
et vindu	*a window*	**vinduet**	*the window*
et bord	*a table*	**bordet**	*the table*
et brød	*a loaf of bread*	**brødet**	*the bread*
et hjem	*a home*	**hjemmet**	*the home*
et hus	*a house*	**huset**	*the house*
et kurs	*a course*	**kurset**	*the course*
et mål	*a voice / language*	**målet**	*the voice / language*
et rom	*a room*	**rommet**	*the room*
et skap	*a cabinet*	**skapet**	*the cabinet*
et skjerf	*a scarf*	**skjerfet**	*the scarf*
et språk	*a language*	**språket**	*the language*
et tegn	*a sign*	**tegnet**	*the sign*
et barn	*a child*	**barnet**	*the child*
et tre	*a tree*	**treet**	*the tree*
Flertall – *plural*			
Ubestemt – *indeterminate*		**Bestemt** – *determinate*	
epler	*(some) apples*	**eplene**	*the apples*
hoteller	*(some) hotels*	**hotellene**	*the hotels*
vinduer	*(some) windows*	**vinduene**	*the windows*
bord	*(some) tables*	**bordene**	*the tables*
brød	*(some) loaves of bread*	**brødene**	*the loaves of bread*
hjem	*(some) homes*	**hjemmene**	*the homes*
hus	*(some) houses*	**husene**	*the houses*
kurs	*(some) courses*	**kursene**	*the courses*
mål	*(some) voices / languages*	**målene**	*the voices / languages*
rom	*(some) rooms*	**rommene**	*the rooms*
skap	*(some) cabinets*	**skapene**	*the cabinets*
skjerf	*(some) scarves*	**skjerfene**	*the scarves*
språk	*(some) languages*	**språkene**	*the languages*
tegn	*(some) signs*	**tegnene**	*the signs*
barn	*(some) children*	**barna**	*the children*
trær	*(some) trees*	**trærne**	*the trees*

Family nouns

Hankjønn – *masculine*			
Entall – *singular*			
Ubestemt – *indeterminate*		**Bestemt** – *determinate*	
en bror	*a brother*	**broren**	*the brother*
en far	*a father*	**faren**	*the father*
en fetter	*a (male) cousin*	**fetteren**	*the (male) cousin*
en forelder	*a parent*	**forelderen**	*the parent*
en mann	*a husband*	**mannen**	*the husband*
en nevø	*a nephew*	**nevøen**	*the nephew*
en onkel	*an uncle*	**onkelen**	*the uncle*
en svigerfar	*a father-in-law*	**svigerfaren**	*the father-in-law*
en svigersønn	*a son-in-law*	**svigersønnen**	*the son-in-law*
en svoger	*a brother-in-law*	**svogeren**	*the brother-in-law*
en sønn	*a son*	**sønnen**	*the son*
Flertall – *plural*			
Ubestemt – *indeterminate*		**Bestemt** – *determinate*	
brødre	*(some) brothers*	**brødrene**	*the brothers*
fedre	*(some) fathers*	**fedrene**	*the fathers*
fettere	*(some male) cousins*	**fetterne**	*the (male) cousins*
foreldre	*(some) parents*	**foreldrene**	*the parents*
menn	*(some) husbands*	**mennene**	*the husbands*
nevøer	*(some) nephews*	**nevøene**	*the nephews*
onkler	*(some) uncles*	**onklene**	*the uncles*
svigerfedre	*(some) fathers-in-law*	**svigerfedrene**	*the fathers-in-law*
svigersønner	*(some) sons-in-law*	**svigersønnene**	*the sons-in-law*
svogere	*(some) brothers-in-law*	**svogerne**	*the brothers-in-law*
sønner	*(some) sons*	**sønnene**	*the sons*

Hunkjønn – *feminine*			
Entall – *singular*			
Ubestemt – *indeterminate*		Bestemt – *determinate*	
ei datter	*a daughter*	**dattera**	*the daughter*
ei kone	*a wife*	**kona**	*the wife*
ei kusine	*a (female) cousin*	**kusina**	*the (female) cousin*
ei mor	*a mother*	**mora**	*the mother*
ei niese	*a niece*	**niesa**	*the niece*
ei svigerdatter	*a daughter-in-law*	**svigerdattera**	*the daughter-in-law*
ei svigerinne	*a sister-in-law*	**svigerinna**	*the sister-in-law*
ei svigermor	*a mother-in-law*	**svigermora**	*the mother-in-law*
ei søster	*a sister*	**søstera**	*the sister*
ei tante	*an aunt*	**tanta**	*the aunt*
Flertall – *plural*			
Ubestemt – *indeterminate*		Bestemt – determinate	
døtre	*(some) daughters*	**døtrene**	*the daughters*
koner	*(some) wives*	**konene**	*the wives*
kusiner	*(some female) cousins*	**kusinene**	*the (female) cousins*
mødre	*(some) mothers*	**mødrene**	*the mothers*
nieser	*(some) nieces*	**niesene**	*the nieces*
svigerdøtre	*(some) daughters-in-law*	**svigerdøtrene**	*the daughters-in-law*
svigerinner	*(some) sisters-in-law*	**svigerinnene**	*the sisters-in-law*
svigermødre	*(some) mothers-in-law*	**svigermødrene**	*the mothers-in-law*
søstre	*(some) sisters*	**søstrene**	*the sisters*
tanter	*(some) aunts*	**tantene**	*the aunts*

Intetkjønn – *neuter*			
Entall – *singular*			
Ubestemt – *indeterminate*		**Bestemt** – *determinate*	
et barn	*a child*	**barnet**	*the child*
et barnebarn	*a grandchild*	**barnebarnet**	*the grandchild*
et søsken	*a sibling*	**søskenet**	*the sibling*
et søskenbarn	*a cousin (both sexes)*	**søskenbarnet**	*the cousin (both sexes)*
Flertall – *plural*			
Ubestemt – *indeterminate*		**Bestemt** – *determinate*	
barn	*(some) children*	**barna**	*the children*
barnebarn	*(some) grandchildren*	**barnebarna**	*the grandchildren*
søsken	*(some) siblings*	**søsknene**	*the siblings*
søskenbarn	*(some) cousins*	**søskenbarna**	*the cousins*

Adjectives

Singular, indefinite		Plural, indefinite (m / f / n)	English
Masculine / feminine	Neuter		
1 The majority of Norwegian adjectives			
dyr	**dyrt**	**dyre**	*expensive*
fin	**fint**	**fine**	*nice*
god	**godt**	**gode**	*good*
grønn	**grønt**	**grønne**	*green*
gul	**gult**	**gule**	*yellow*
kald	**kaldt**	**kalde**	*cold*
pen	**pent**	**pene**	*beautiful*
varm	**varmt**	**varme**	*warm*
2 Plurisyllabic adjectives and adjectives of nationality ending in -sk			
engelsk	**engelsk**	**engelske**	*English*
fantastisk	**fantastisk**	**fantastiske**	*fantastic*
norsk	**norsk**	**norske**	*Norwegian*
3 Monosyllabic adjectives ending in -sk			
fersk	**ferskt**	**ferske**	*fresh*
frisk	**friskt**	**friske**	*healthy*
rask	**raskt**	**raske**	*quick*
4 Adjectives ending in -ig			
billig	**billig**	**billige**	*cheap*
kjedelig	**kjedelig**	**kjedelige**	*boring*
5 Monosyllabic adjectives ending in a (tonic / with accent) vowel			
blå	**blått**	**blå / blåe**	*blue*
fri	**fritt**	**frie**	*free*
ny	**nytt**	**nye**	*new*
6 Adjectives ending in -e			
ekte	**ekte**	**ekte**	*original*
moderne	**moderne**	**moderne**	*modern*
7 Adjectives which come from a participle			
sjarmerende	**sjarmerende**	**sjarmerende**	*charming*
spennende	**spennende**	**spennende**	*thrilling*
8 Adjectives containing double consonants			
gammel	**gammelt**	**gamle**	*old*
vakker	**vakkert**	**vakre**	*beautiful*
9 Adjectives ending in -en			
voksen	**voksent**	**voksne**	*adult*
sliten	**slitent**	**slitne**	*tired*

Comparatives and superlatives

Adjective – base form, singular	Comparative	Superlative	English
1 The majority of Norwegian adjectives			
dyr	**dyrere**	**dyrest**	*expensive*
enkel	**enklere**	**enklest**	*easy*
fin	**finere**	**finest**	*nice*
kald	**kaldere**	**kaldest**	*cold*
morsom	**morsommere**	**morsomst**	*funny*
pen	**penere**	**penest**	*beautiful*
varm	**varmere**	**varmest**	*warm*
2 Plurisyllabic adjectives and adjectives of nationality ending in -sk			
engelsk	**mer engelsk**	**mest engelsk**	*English*
fantastisk	**mer fantastisk**	**mest fantastisk**	*fantastic*
norsk	**mer norsk**	**mest norsk**	*Norwegian*
praktisk	**mer praktisk**	**mest praktisk**	*practical*
3 Monosyllabic adjectives ending in -sk			
fersk	**ferskere**	**ferskest**	*fresh*
frisk	**friskere**	**friskest**	*healthy*
rask	**raskere**	**raskest**	*quick*
4 Adjectives ending in -ig			
billig	**billigere**	**billigst**	*cheap*
kjedelig	**kjedeligere**	**kjedeligst**	*boring*
vanskelig	**vanskeligere**	**vanskeligst**	*difficult*
viktig	**viktigere**	**viktigst**	*important*
5 Monosyllabic adjectives ending in a (tonic / with accent) vowel			
fri	**friere**	**friest**	*free*
ny	**nyere**	**nyest**	*new*
6 Adjectives ending in -e			
ekte	**mer ekte**	**mest ekte**	*original*
moderne	**mer moderne**	**mest moderne**	*modern*
rotete	**mer rotete**	**mest rotete**	*untidy*
7 Adjectives which come from a participle			
sjarmerende	**mer sjarmerende**	**mest sjarmerende**	*charming*
spennende	**mer spennende**	**mest spennende**	*thrilling*
8 Adjectives containing double consonants			
lett	**lettere**	**lettest**	*easy*
snill	**snillere**	**snillest**	*kind*
vakker	**vakrere**	**vakrest**	*beautiful*
9 Adjectives ending in -en			
sliten	**mer sliten**	**mest sliten**	*tired*
voksen	**mer voksen**	**mest voksen**	*adult*
10 Adjectives which contain the letter u			
tung	**tyngre**	**tyngst**	*heavy*
ung	**yngre**	**yngst**	*young*

Irregular comparatives and superlatives

Adjective / adverb	Comparative	Superlative	English
dårlig / ille	**verre**	**verst**	*bad*
få	**færre**	**færrest**	*few*
gammel	**eldre**	**eldst**	*old*
gjerne	**heller**	**helst**	*gladly*
god / bra	**bedre**	**best**	*good / well*
lang	**lengre**	**lengst**	*long*
lite	**mindre**	**minst**	*less*
mange	**flere**	**flest**	*many*
mye	**mer**	**mest**	*much*
stor	**større**	**størst**	*big*

Verb tenses

IRREGULAR VERBS

Infinitive (*infinitiv*)	Present (*presens*)	Simple past (*preteritum*)	Present perfect (*presens perfektum*)	English
å være	**er**	**var**	**har vært**	*to be*
å bli	**blir**	**ble**	**har blitt**	*to become / stay*
å gjøre	**gjør**	**gjorde**	**har gjort**	*to do*
å drikke	**drikker**	**drakk**	**har drukket**	*to drink*
å falle	**faller**	**falt**	**har falt**	*to fall*
å gi	**gir**	**ga**	**har gitt**	*to give*
å dra	**drar**	**dro**	**har dratt**	*to go / travel*
å gå	**går**	**gikk**	**har gått**	*to go / walk*
å be	**ber**	**ba**	**har bedt**	*to pray*
å si	**sier**	**sa**	**har sagt**	*to say*
å se	**ser**	**så**	**har sett**	*to see*
å stå	**står**	**sto**	**har stått**	*to stand*
å forstå	**forstår**	**forsto**	**har forstått**	*to understand*

GROUP 1

Infinitive (*infinitiv*)	Present (*presens*)	Simple past (*preteritum*)	Present perfect (*presens perfektum*)	English
å fiske	**fisker**	**fisket**	**har fisket**	*to fish*
å hate	**hater**	**hatet**	**har hatet**	*to hate*
å pakke	**pakker**	**pakket**	**har pakket**	*to pack*
å snakke	**snakker**	**snakket**	**har snakket**	*to talk / to speak*
å rydde	**rydder**	**ryddet**	**har ryddet**	*to tidy*
å vente	**venter**	**ventet**	**har ventet**	*to wait*
å vaske	**vasker**	**vasket**	**har vasket**	*to wash*

GROUP 2

Infinitive (*infinitiv*)	Present (*presens*)	Simple past (*preteritum*)	Present perfect (*presens perfektum*)	English
å besøke	**besøker**	**besøkte**	**har besøkt**	*to visit*
å betale	**betaler**	**betalte**	**har betalt**	*to pay*
å fortelle	**forteller**	**fortalte**	**har fortalt**	*to tell*
å glemme	**glemmer**	**glemte**	**har glemt**	*to forget*
å høre	**hører**	**hørte**	**har hørt**	*to hear*
å leke	**leker**	**lekte**	**har lekt**	*to play*
å lese	**leser**	**leste**	**har lest**	*to read / to study*
å reise	**reiser**	**reiste**	**har reist**	*to travel*
å spille	**spiller**	**spilte**	**har spilt**	*to play*
å spise	**spiser**	**spiste**	**har spist**	*to eat*
å spørre	**spør**	**spurte**	**har spurt**	*to ask*
å vise	**viser**	**viste**	**har vist**	*to show*
å vite	**vet**	**visste**	**har visst**	*to know*

GROUP 3

Infinitive (*infinitiv*)	Present (*presens*)	Simple past (*preteritum*)	Present perfect (*presens perfektum*)	English
å bøye	**bøyer**	**bøyde**	**har bøyd**	*to bend*
å leve	**lever**	**levde**	**har levd**	*to live*
å leie	**leier**	**leide**	**har leid**	*to rent*
å prøve	**prøver**	**prøvde**	**har prøvd**	*to try*
å veie	**veier**	**veide**	**har veid**	*to weigh*

GROUP 4

Infinitive (*infinitiv*)	Present (*presens*)	Simple past (*preteritum*)	Present perfect (*presens perfektum*)	English
å tro	**tror**	**trodde**	**har trodd**	*to believe*
å ha	**har**	**hadde**	**har hatt**	*to have*
å bo	**bor**	**bodde**	**ha bodd**	*to live (inhabit)*
å nå	**når**	**nådde**	**har nådd**	*to reach*
å snø	**snør**	**snødde**	**har snødd**	*to snow*

MODAL VERBS

Infinitive (*infinitiv*)	Present (*presens*)	Simple past (*preteritum*)	Present perfect (*presens perfektum*)	English
å kunne	**kan**	**kunne**	**har kunnet**	*can*
å måtte	**må**	**måtte**	**har måttet**	*must*
å burde	**bør**	**burde**	**har burdet**	*should*
å ville	**vil**	**ville**	**har villet**	*want*
å skulle	**skal**	**skulle**	**har skullet**	*will / (shall)*

Norwegian–English

aften (en)	*evening*
agurk (en)	*cucumber*
amerikaner (en)	*American*
aprikos (en)	*apricot*
april	*April*
arabisk	*Arabic*
artisjokk (en)	*artichoke*
aubergine (en)	*aubergine*
august	*August*
badedrakt (en)	*swimsuit*
badekåpe (ei / en)	*bathrobe*
banan (en)	*banana*
bh (en)	*bra*
bjørnebær (et)	*blackberry*
bluse (ei)	*blouse*
blå	*blue*
blåbær (et)	*blueberry*
bobledress (en)	*quilted overall (commonly worn in Norway)*
boblejakke (ei / en)	*quilted jacket*
bra	*well*
bringebær (et)	*raspberry*
bukse (en) / bukser	*trouser(s)*
dag (en)	*day*
dansk	*Danish*
danske (en)	*Dane*
desember	*December*
drikke	*drinks*
drue (en / ei)	*grapes*
engelsk	*English*
engelskmann (en)	*Englishman*
eple (et)	*apple*
ertestuing (en / ei)	*mashed / creamed peas*
februar	*February*
fennikel (en)	*fennel*
fersken (en)	*peach*
fin	*fine*
finne (en)	*Finn*

finsk	*Finnish*
fint	*fine*
fiolett	*violet*
fransk	*French*
franskmann (en)	*Frenchman / Frenchwoman*
fredag (en)	*Friday*
frukt (en / ei)	*fruit*
færøysk	*Faroese*
genser (en)	*sweater / jumper*
god	*good*
godt	*good*
grønn	*green*
grå	*gray*
gul	*yellow*
gulrot (en / ei)	*carrot*
ha det	*goodbye*
hagle (en / ei)	*hail*
hallo	*hi / hello*
hanske (en)	*glove(s)*
hasselnøtt (en / ei)	*hazelnut*
hatt (en)	*hat*
hei	*hi / hello*
hindi	*Hindi*
hvit	*white*
hvitløk (en)	*garlic*
høst (en)	*autumn / fall*
i dag	*today*
i går	*yesterday*
inder (en)	*Indian*
ire (en)	*Irishman / Irishwoman*
irsk	*Irish*
is (en)	*ice*
islandsk	*Icelandic*
islending (en)	*Icelander*
italiener (en)	*Italian*
italiensk	*Italian*
jakke (ei)	*jacket*
januar	*January*
jordbær (et)	*strawberry*
juice (en)	*juice*
juli	*July*
juni	*June*
kaldt	*cold*

kineser (en) | *Chinese*
kinesisk | *Chinese*
kirsebær (et) | *cherry*
kjole (en) | *dress*
klær | *clothes*
kveld (en) | *evening*
kåpe (ei / en) | *coat*
lilla | *lilac*
lue (ei) | *beret*
lyn (et) | *lightning*
lørdag (en) | *Saturday*
mai | *May*
mandag (en) | *Monday*
mars | *March*
mat (en) | *food*
melk (en) | *milk*
morgen (en) | *morning*
multe (en) | *cloudberry*
måne (en) | *moon*
måned (en) | *month*
natt (en / ei) | *night*
nederlandsk | *Dutch*
nederlender (en) | *Dutchman / Dutchwoman*
nordmann (en) | *Norwegian*
norsk | *Norwegian*
november | *November*
nøtt (en / ei) | *nut*
oktober | *October*
ola-bukse / jeans (ei / en) | *jeans*
onsdag (en) | *Wednesday*
oransje | *orange*
polakk (en) | *Pole*
polsk | *Polish*
portugiser (en) | *Portuguese*
portugisisk | *Portuguese*
potet (en) | *potato*
pære (en / ei) | *pear*
regn (et) | *rain*
regnjakke (ei) | *rain jacket*
rosa | *pink*
russer (en) | *Russian*
russisk | *Russian*
ryggsekk (en) | *backpack*

rød	*red*
samisk	*Sami*
september	*September*
shorts (en)	*shorts*
sist	*last time*
sjal (et)	*shawl*
skjerf (et)	*scarf*
skjorte (ei)	*shirt*
skjørt (et)	*skirt*
sko (en)	*shoe(s)*
skotsk	*Scottish*
skotte (en)	*Scot*
snart	*soon*
snø (en)	*snow*
sokk (en)	*sock*
sol (en / ei)	*sun*
sommer (en)	*summer*
spanjol (en)	*Spaniard*
spansk	*Spanish*
spinat (en)	*spinach*
squash (en)	*squash*
strømpe (ei / en)	*stocking*
strømpebukse (en)	*tights*
støvel (en)	*boot(s)*
svart	*black*
sveitser (en)	*Swiss*
svensk	*Swedish*
svenske (en)	*Swede*
søndag (en)	*Sunday*
takk	*thanks*
tirsdag (en)	*Tuesday*
tomat (en)	*tomato*
torden (en)	*thunder*
torsdag (en)	*Thursday*
truse (ei / en)	*panties*
t-skjorte (ei)	*T-shirt*
tysk	*German*
tysker (en)	*German*
tyttebær (et)	*lingonberry*
tåke (en / ei)	*fog*
ullgenser (en)	*woollen sweater*
undertøy (et / --)	*underwear*
vann (et)	*water*

vannmelon (en)	*watermelon*
varmt	*warm*
veske (ei / en)	*bag*
vin (en)	*wine*
vind (en)	*wind*
vinter (en)	*winter*
vott (en)	*mitten(s)*
vår (en)	*spring*
waliser (en)	*Welshman / Welshwoman*
walisisk	*Welsh*
øl (en)	*beer*
østerriker (en)	*Austrian*
å bli	*to become / to stay*
å blåse	*to blow*
å dra	*to go (using mode of transport, not driving)*
å drikke	*to drink*
å dusje	*to shower*
å fly	*to fly*
å fryse	*to freeze*
å gjøre	*to do*
å gå	*to walk*
å kjøre	*to drive*
å komme	*to come*
å lage	*to make*
å ligge	*to lie (down)*
å lyne	*to strike with lightning*
å regne	*to rain*
å reise	*to travel*
å sitte	*to sit*
å skinne	*to shine*
å snø	*to snow*
å spise	*to eat*
å stå	*to stand*
å svette	*to sweat*
å ta	*to take*
å tordne	*to thunder*
årstid (en)	*season*

English–Norwegian

American	**amerikaner** (en)
apple	**eple** (et)
apricot	**aprikos** (en)
April	**april**
Arabic	**arabisk**
artichoke	**artisjokk** (en)
aubergine	**aubergine** (en)
August	**august**
Austrian	**østerriker** (en)
autumn / fall	**høst** (en)
backpack	**ryggsekk** (en)
bag	**veske** (ei / en)
banana	**banan** (en)
bathrobe	**badekåpe** (ei / en)
beer	**øl** (en)
beret	**lue** (ei)
black	**svart**
blackberry	**bjørnebær** (et)
blouse	**bluse** (ei)
blue	**blå**
blueberry	**blåbær** (et)
boot(s)	**støvel** (en)
bra	**bh** (en)
carrot	**gulrot** (en / ei)
cherry	**kirsebær** (et)
Chinese	**kineser** (en)
Chinese	**kinesisk**
clothes	**klær**
coat	**kåpe** (ei / en)
cold	**kaldt**
cucumber	**agurk** (en)
Dane	**danske** (en)
Danish	**dansk**
day	**dag** (en)
December	**desember**
dress	**kjole** (en)
drinks	**drikke** (en / ei)
Dutch	**nederlandsk**

Dutchman / Dutchwoman	**nederlender** (en)
English	**engelsk**
Englishman	**engelskmann** (en)
evening	**aften** (en), **kveld** (en)
Faroese	**færøysk**
February	**februar**
fennel	**fennikel** (en)
fine	**fin / fint**
Finn	**finne** (en)
Finnish	**finsk**
fog	**tåke** (en / ei)
food	**mat** (en)
French	**fransk**
Frenchman / Frenchwoman	**franskmann** (en)
Friday	**fredag** (en)
fruit	**frukt** (en / ei)
German	**tysk**
German	**tysker** (en)
glove(s)	**hanske** (en)
good	**god**
good	**godt**
goodbye	**ha det**
grapes	**drue** (en / ei)
green	**grønn**
gray	**grå**
hail	**hagle** (en / ei)
hat	**hatt** (en)
hazelnut	**hasselnøtt** (en / ei)
hi / hello	**hallo / hei**
Hindi	**hindi**
ice	**is** (en)
Icelander	**islending** (en)
Icelandic	**islandsk**
Indian	**inder** (en)
Irish	**irsk**
Irishman / Irishwoman	**ire** (en)
Italian	**italiener** (en)
Italian	**italiensk**
jacket	**jakke** (ei)
January	**januar**
jeans	**ola-bukse / jeans** (ei / en)
juice	**juice** (en)

July	**juli**
June	**juni**
last time	**sist**
lightning	**lyn** (et)
lilac	**lilla**
lingonberry	**tyttebær** (et)
March	**mars**
May	**mai**
milk	**melk** (en)
mitten(s)	**vott** (en)
Monday	**mandag** (en)
month	**måned** (en)
moon	**måne** (en)
morning	**morgen** (en)
cloudberry	**multe** (en)
night	**natt** (en / ei)
Norwegian	**nordmann** (en)
Norwegian	**norsk**
November	**november**
nut	**nøtt** (en / ei)
October	**oktober**
orange	**oransje**
panties	**truse** (ei / en)
peach	**fersken** (en)
pear	**pære** (en / ei)
pink	**rosa**
Pole	**polakk** (en)
Polish	**polsk**
Portuguese	**portugiser** (en)
Portuguese	**portugisisk**
potato	**potet** (en)
quilted jacket	**boblejakke** (ei / en)
quilted overall (commonly worn in Norway)	**bobledress** (en)
rain	**regn** (et)
rain jacket	**regnjakke** (ei)
raspberry	**bringebær** (et)
red	**rød**
Russian	**russer** (en)
Russian	**russisk**
Sami	**samisk**
Saturday	**lørdag** (en)
scarf	**skjerf** (et)
Scot	**skotte** (en)

Scottish	**skotsk**
season	**årstid** (en)
September	**september**
shawl	**sjal** (et)
shirt	**skjorte** (ei)
shoe(s)	**sko** (en)
shorts	**shorts** (en)
skirt	**skjørt** (et)
snow	**snø** (en)
sock	**sokk** (en)
soon	**snart**
Spaniard	**spanjol** (en)
Spanish	**spansk**
spinach	**spinat** (en)
spring	**vår** (en)
squash	**squash** (en)
stocking	**strømpe** (ei / en)
strawberry	**jordbær** (et)
summer	**sommer** (en)
sun	**sol** (en / ei)
Sunday	**søndag** (en)
sweater / jumper	**genser** (en)
Swede	**svenske** (en)
Swedish	**svensk**
swimsuit	**badedrakt** (en)
Swiss	**sveitser** (en)
thanks	**takk**
thunder	**torden** (en)
Thursday	**torsdag** (en)
tights	**strømpebukse** (en)
to become / to stay	**å bli**
to blow	**å blåse**
to come	**å komme**
to do	**å gjøre**
to drink	**å drikke**
to drive	**å kjøre**
to eat	**å spise**
to fly	**å fly**
to freeze	**å fryse**
to go (using a means of transport but not driving it)	**å dra**
to lie (down)	**å ligge**
to make	**å lage**
to rain	**å regne**

to shine	**å skinne**
to shower	**å dusje**
to sit	**å sitte**
to snow	**å snø**
to stand	**å stå**
to strike with lightning	**å lyne**
to sweat	**å svette**
to take	**å ta**
to thunder	**å tordne**
to travel	**å reise**
to walk	**å gå**
today	**i dag**
tomato	**tomat** (en)
trouser(s)	**bukse** (en) **/ bukser**
T-shirt	**t-skjorte** (ei)
Tuesday	**tirsdag** (en)
underwear	**undertøy** (et)
violet	**fiolett**
warm	**varmt**
water	**vann** (et)
watermelon	**vannmelon** (en)
Wednesday	**onsdag** (en)
well	**bra**
Welsh	**walisisk**
Welshman / Welshwoman	**waliser** (en)
white	**hvit**
wind	**vind** (en)
wine	**vin** (en)
winter	**vinter** (en)
woollen sweater	**ullgenser** (en)
yellow	**gul**
yesterday	**i går**

Image credits

Illustrations by Barking Dog Art

xix – Kommunal-og distriktsdepartementet/Planavdelingen, Public domain, via Wikimedia Commons

Unit 7 – © Dasha Petrenko/Shutterstock

Can-do statements

UNIT	CEFR level	ACTFL level	CAN-DO STATEMENTS
UNIT 1	**A1**	**Novice High**	I can introduce myself and others and can ask and answer questions about personal details such as where someone lives.
UNIT 2	**A1**	**Novice High**	I can understand and use familiar everyday expressions and very basic phrases. I can get an idea of simple informational material. I can talk about personal details (name, address, languages spoken). I can handle negative forms.
UNIT 3	**A1**	**Novice High**	I can understand and use familiar everyday expressions and very basic phrases. I can handle numbers and get an idea of simple informational material. I can fill in forms with personal details (name, age, address, registration) of myself and others.
UNIT 4	**A1**	**Novice High**	I can talk about family relations and can handle 'irregular' names. I can name months, days and seasons. I can handle possessives and can ask what things are called in Norwegian.
UNIT 5	**A1**	**Novice High**	I can handle quantities, qualities (colors, sizes, etc.) and costs, and can ask people for things.
UNIT 6	**A1**	**Novice High**	I can talk about time and daily routine. I can handle times of the day and days of the week. I can use several kinds of verbs to describe movement.

UNIT 7	**A1**	**Novice High**	I can order a meal. I can give and follow short, simple directions and follow written instructions.
UNIT 8	**A1**	**Novice High**	I can get simple information about travel and the use of public transport, give directions and buy tickets. I can write short, simple notes. I can find specific, predictable information in simple everyday material such as timetables. I can talk about feelings and illnesses. I can refer to different body parts.
UNIT 9	**A1 / A2**	**Novice High / Intermediate Low**	**(A1)** I can handle past tenses. I can describe someone's physical appearance and greet people on different holidays. **(A2)** I can write short, simple notes and messages relating to matters in areas of immediate need.
UNIT 10	**A1**	**Novice High / Intermediate Low**	**(A1)** I can talk about the weather. I can handle simple information about pastimes and hobbies. I can describe usual actions. **(A2)** I can write about everyday aspects of my environment. I can understand short, simple texts containing the highest frequency vocabulary. I can use simple descriptive language to make brief statements about and compare objects.